When God Goes Silent

Living Life Without God's Voice

When God Goes Silent

Living Life Without God's Voice

PAULA A. PRICE, PH.D.

Flaming Vision Publications

Revised Edition

©2008 in the United States of America

Unless otherwise indicated, all scriptural quotations are from the King James Version of the Bible.

When God Goes Silent: Living Life Without God's Voice

Published by Flaming Vision Publications

Tulsa, Oklahoma 74136

ISBN 1-886288-39-9

Dedication

This book is dedicated to the memory of my mother, Reverend Dorothy C. Thomas, a prayer warrior the world will sorely miss. She went home to be with the Lord February 21, 2010. Of all the things to remember about my mom, two stand out most of all. They are her ceaseless encouragement and her passionate fellowship with the Lord. I do not know of a single person who spent more time in the presence of Jesus Christ or who was hungrier for His communion than she was.

Table of Contents

Preface

Three things await you as you read this book. The first is of it being a precious gift from the Spirit of Christ to this generation. *When God Goes Silent* is a gift to those members who yearn for a deeper and more vibrant communion with the Lord. The other treasure is wisdom. This guide shares with you who wish to step up your relationship with the Lord how to get God talking, and how to enjoy delightful conversations with Him, whenever. This book helps you detect the true God from false gods. The third insight this book provides is for those who once enjoyed exciting communion with God and no longer do so. It gives some practical tips on how to revive your relationship with the Lord after He has gone silent for some time.

Of all the prized gifts of salvation bestowed by the Lord upon His church as part of His new covenant ratified by the shed blood of Jesus Christ, fellowship and communion with the Most High is the most precious. A guide like this one helps you see how to get the most from both your fellowship and your times of communion with the Lord your God. Specially written to those who welcome God being Himself with them, you will appreciate most of all is how to see and relate to God as He is. With the explanations and suggestions given here, you will learn how to learn God's voice, understand His thoughts, and keep the communications lines between you and the Almighty open. For you who crave a close and refreshing union with God, this information is vital since the last thing you want is silence between you and your God.

Many people crave rich fellowship with the Lord, but not everyone quite understands what that is or what it involves. Few people will argue that communion without communication is impossible. The problem is most people believe that expecting to or actually conversing with the Lord is impossible and foolish. So they opt for a silent relationship with any unknown spiritual being that strikes their fancy. Early in my walk with Jesus, I found that was not for me.

While it is true that countless souls appreciate the mysticism of sitting in their god's presence saying and thinking nothing. But, I could never serve a god I could not reach. Others may disagree, but to me interaction with the Lord and Possessor of my soul is very important and I need Him to respond to me. I could never venerate a silent god or worship a handmade one. When it comes to communing with the Lord, I expect it to be two way, which is why I serve the living God today. I want a lively relationship with the one I will spend forever with, a relationship that gives and gives back. A god that cannot respond to me is useless.

It is true that some love mystically sitting in an invisible being's presence for hours or days at a time and say nothing. In fact, several religions are based upon that very thing, but to me it is very one-sided and empty. Still, millions of souls rest their entire spiritual experience on religious silence, taking pleasure in mutely exploring the mysteries of nothingness. It sounds very pious, but such exchanges leave only the worshipper to assume benefits from the encounter. Others, if there are any, must take at face value what the mute soul says happened from the experience, or if anything happened at all. That, however, is not how the Lord Almighty communes. The Most High God loves to talk, to share, to hear and to be heard. Remember these four things as you read this book and your interactions with Him will soar day after day, year after years all the way throughout eternity.

Introduction

To paint a picture for you of what *When God Goes Silent* addresses, I am reminded of a lunch I recently had with my prophets. One of the youngest trainees shared a word that she received from the Lord in response to a question she asked of Him. She said the Lord Jesus answered her question with these words. Calling her by name He said, "I say so much and you listen so little." Typical of God, He cut through to the heart of the matter and addressed pretty much all of her questions at once, revealing in a single word why His counsel was not working for her. The problem was not God talking, but her listening. I was as impressed with His response as she was stunned, remarking to myself how ingeniously the Lord's answer to one person spoke to everyone at the table and answered their questions too. In fact, I was a bit pricked at heart myself because His simple sounding statement spoke volumes to me as well. It is true; God does say so much, and we do listen so very little.

Our Lord wants to talk, He wants to teach us and guide us, and He wants to get us through life one crisis and defeat, blessing and victory at a time. He wants us to grow in Him, to need Him, to pursue His wisdom, and once we grab hold of Him, He yearns for us to cling to Him. God is passionate about conversing with us, and yet, incredibly many saints are just happy to talk *at* Him and never *with* Him. They are comfortable with assuming He heard them and hurriedly tell themselves what they want Him to say instead of waiting for Him to speak on His own. People find it difficult to accept that the Lord has His own mind, His own way of thinking and living life (His and ours). He has His own wisdom to impart to us if we would just stop doing His thinking for Him. Sadly, it seems far too many Christians are afraid to trust the Lord to speak for Himself and would rather act on what they would tell themselves to do if indeed they were God; how unfortunate. God wants to speak for Himself and be heard and obeyed on His own terms. He prefers to be enjoyed in the ways that please Him and not just us. That is what must happen if we want to keep Him talking and actively involved in our lives. Listening, heeding, obeying, and revering God will keep Him chatting with you all the time. All of these are what this book reveals to you.

Also, you will appreciate is its indepth treatment of the Holy Spirit, because without the Holy Spirit there can be no communication or communion with God who is spirit. Chapter 2 gives a revelation about the Holy Spirit that promises to revolutionize how you see God's Spirit in your life from now on. It will also transform how you access and commune with the Godhead, which can only be through His Spirit. To comprehend the revelations on the Holy Spirit correctly, think about this. Countless souls in God's kingdom, question who the Holy Spirit is and what makes Him who He is to us in this world, and why He is necessary to their Christianity. They wonder, "Is He God or what? If He is God, how does one relate to Him being spirit and all?" They wonder how communion with the Holy Spirit differs from our fellowship with God the Father and God the Son. And then there is that thorny issue of the Godhead, traditionally called the Trinity. What is that three-in-one thing all about anyway? How can three people be one and one person be three people at the same time? All of this begins to make sense when you grasp the essence of the Holy Spirit. In the meantime, to get started, look over Isaiah 48:16 to meet the Three-in-One in action. In addition, two of them show up in Luke 2:25-28 and the third one Person of the Godhead, Yahweh, surfaces in verse 29. Luke 3:22 shows them synchronizing again. Of course, there is the famous Great Commission in Matthew 28:18-20, and let us not overlook 1 John 5:7. Luke 4:18, brought forward from Isaiah 61:1-3, and Luke 11:13 that have Jesus — God the Son — referring to God the Father and God the Holy Spirit as simultaneous and yet distinct partners with Him in His earthly ministry. Further insight may be gained from reading John 14:14-18 where the Savior subtly tells His disciples that they are about to receive the fullness of the Godhead bodily as members of His personage. John the Apostle underscores this miraculous event in John 15:26, 16:13 of his gospel. Galatians 4:6, Hebrews 9:14, and 1 John 4:2 enlighten us further on the mystery of the Godhead's *godness*.

What all of these passages share, is their portrayal of the Godhead at work in heaven and on earth. Collectively, they legitimize the Holy Spirit as equally God, sketching for us how one member of the Trinity never acts apart from or independent of the others. So you can rest assured that if you please the Father, you have pleased His Son and vice versa, and when you connect with God the Father and God the Son through the Holy Spirit, you have contacted the entire Godhead. He is the only way to enter the presence of God and capture His ear. What a blessing.

Another question often posed about God is, "How are the three equally one and what holds them all together?" The answer to the first question is the Holy Spirit. Chapter two explains how and why. Reviewing Colossians 1:2 opens it up more as does 1 Timothy 3:16, which says, "Great is the mystery of Godliness". What holds the Almighty three in one all together? The Holy Spirit, according to Isaiah 48:16.

A final thought on the Holy Spirit and the Godhead is Jesus Christ, the Messiah, our cornerstone and stumbling rock of offense. No other person in history has ever or will ever be more controversial. Nothing riles up souls like Jesus Christ. It does not matter if they are Christians or anti-christs; the mention of His name finds no neutralists. But who is Jesus besides the Savior precious and loathed, the Son of God prized and envied? *When God Goes Silent* answers this as well. In a word, Jesus Christ is God's portability and physicality. He is how the Almighty, who keeps all creation together and fills all in all, manifests Himself locally in various places. The Holy Spirit, on the other hand, does

15

the exact opposite. He is how the Almighty universalizes Himself to be everywhere present at once. This is just a taste of what you will enjoy from the wealth of wisdom and nuggets of truth to be found in this book. After you have finished reading it, you will find things will never be the same between you and the Lord, and your fellowship with Him will break barrier after barrier as long as you remain on earth.

Use this book as a potent addition to any spiritual education and training classes. It augments well prophetic training programs, Holy Spirit classes, and teachings on how to hear and respond to God's voice. Use it as well as part of your ministerial readiness curriculum. There is a workbook to go along with this book to facilitate a trainer's or a moderator's organized instruction in this all important subject.

Chapter One

Passionate vs. Dutiful Worship

ou know, most people in the world live and die never hearing the voice of God, the true and living God that is. Others who have their spiritual ears awakened by another god find themselves caught in the grip of a false religion rolling around on the afterlife roulette wheel. They spend their time on earth being led by a deceiving spirit that implies blessings that really aim to secure their doom. Aside from this group are the restrained, super intellectual, and the non-emotional Christians. These people know God talks—some have even heard Him speak once or twice—but they prefer to keep God and spirituality at a safe distance. Their "life under the sun" philosophy believes that anything apart from the five senses is to be shunned. God must communicate with them by instinct, intuition, and perception, what we know to be "hunches", or

frequently described as "something told me." None of these are wrong or insignificant; they are just limiting.

What you read here however, is for those who currently enjoy rich, vibrant communion and fellowship with the Lord, those who want to have such a relationship with the Almighty, or those who used to have that type of relationship with Him and wonder what happened to it. *When God Goes Silent* is also for you who are pressing God for a deeper intimacy and you who want to understand how to get and keep His ear. God's involvement in your life is more important to you than anything else.

Everything you read here is aimed at helping Christians establish and maintain a more than passive, see-you-in-the-afterlife relationship with their Heavenly Father and the Savior Jesus Christ. This material means to encourage and admonish those presently reaping the benefits of rich and open communications with the Lord on how to keep your heavenly relations with Him open. The type of communications with the Lord that is fueled by fertile interpersonal interactions with the God of Heaven and not just the exercise of spiritual gifts to retrieve divine information or exploit covenant blessings. Spiritual gifts exercised under these conditions merely want to use God's grace as a supply line to human desires. Their sole objective is to get earthly needs met or to show off. That is not what sincere love for God settles for or chases. Sincere love for God penetrates His heart and soul and moves Him to get and remain intimately involved with you as an active partner in life. Spiritual affections on this order impose very few boundaries on either side. It is pure and ardent communion that goes way past maneuvering God's covenant and scriptures to get what one wants from Him. Such intimacy links up with Him, follows His lead and has the respect that only pure love has for the object of its affection. The self serving worshipper cannot fathom such a union with the Lord. Their self-motivated spiritual offerings are laden with requests and pleas that reach out to the Almighty their way. Such devotions give no consideration to what He needs, feels, desires, or even requires. Exchanges with the Lord on these bases do not seek to nor are able to serve or benefit Him; they only want Him to indulge them. It is a primitive faith that is no different from what He deals with everyday, age to age, from the unregenerate world. Unions with the Lord of this ilk are fleshly and self-serving. They are maintained by worshippers bent on using the Most High to obtain the desires of their own hearts. What they bring to Him, can or are willing to give in return never enters into it at all. The zenith of such attitudes is a quick material return for minimal spiritual effort, nothing more.

None of this is to say that people cannot be blessed who have never heard the voice of the Lord, or that not hearing God's voice makes you a carnal Christian or not His child. Neither of these is true, nor do they make up the underlying messages of this book. *When God Goes Silent* merely wants to open up another dimension of God for the serious seeker, who is determined to worship God the way He responds to best. That is with worship and fellowship that approaches Him on His terms and not ours. Essentially, that is what Jesus sought to convey when He spoke

John 4:24. Here you will get solid ways to understand what God wants, how He wants to be treated, and what will close His ears and mind to us. These issues are voiced about Him incessantly, perhaps more than any others. Often people get halted in their Christian faith and walk because they simply cannot figure out what the Lord wants and how to get Him to respond to them when they reach out to Him. Far too many Christians are at a loss to say or comprehend what will make Him move, what will touch His heart on their behalf, and why He prefers to be so enigmatic when they need Him to be plain. In every fruitful way, God's perspective on what it means to be intimate with Him is examined and explained for you as you read on. This wisdom shows you how empty it is to pursue intimacy with the Lord only to acquire His provisions with profiles of the most common types of worshippers who are inclined to do so.

For the record, worshippers generally fall into two major groups: the passionate and the dutiful. The latter group, the dutiful, can only connect with the Lord's materiality. They find His spirituality too much to handle[1]. If that is sufficient for them, God be praised. The passionate on the other hand, want to tap into the Lord's wealth of spiritual blessings first because they are convinced it is a sure way to access and retain His material

---

[1] See 1 Corinthians 2:13. Study the word for *comparing* from the Strong's G4793. You will see that it refers to judging one thing in connection with another by combining spiritual ideas with their corresponding behavioral expressions. It speaks to contrasting one thing with another to arrive at both similarities and distinctions. For some people the work that goes into doing this consistently is just too great an effort. Connect your insights with 1 Corinthians 3:1.

blessings[2] without gimmicks. For this group, God's spirituality is craved as much as His materiality, and with some of them even moreso. Those with this mind pursue the Lord with a holy passion that is as equally concerned about His righteousness as they are about their own spiritual enjoyment. For many Christians this is not always the case. For the genuine and passionate, Jesus is their model and motivation. They take to heart the spirit and the letter of Hebrews 7:26 and 1 John 2:6. Their spiritual passion comes from a belief that the Lord's needs and experiences are just as important as their own, if not more. With you, I share the following wisdom from God's mysteries, starting with revering the Holy Spirit, because scripture tells us that it all begins with the Holy Spirit.

---

[2] See the context in which Jesus spoke Matthew 6:33: "But seek ye first the kingdom of God, and his righteousness; and all these things shall be added unto you".

Chapter Two

Revere the Holy Spirit

The first thing you need to know about communing with God is that it is only through the Holy Spirit. That is what our Savior teaches in John 4:23, 24. The second thing you should know is that you must be born again to commune with the true and living God. See John 1:12, 13; 3:16, 17. John 3:31; John 8:23; Luke 1:35.

Scripture makes this plain that God can talk to or through anyone. This is presented most of all in its prophetic writings. The whole of the Gospels makes the case. God, who incarnated in the Person of His Son Jesus Christ, came to earth in the form of a man. After paying the price for our sins, He left us a Helper and Comforter to indwell the redeemed so that we can experience Him continually and remain in constant contact with our heavenly Father. That Helper and Comforter is the Holy Spirit who transported Jesus, the Son of God, to earth, which is what made Him sinless and God in this world as well as His own. It is through these events that Christians are able to know God and distinguish Him from the fallen angels that imitate Him to steal His glory and worship. For the early church, this necessity could have been difficult to grasp since all but the Jewish converts were coming to Christ from polytheism[3] and pantheism[4]. Well, perhaps not, since everyone back then lived under a wholly divine culture where spiritual beings immediately and conspicuously governed and manipulated their world. Today, it could be just as hard to detect their existence and mischief if it were not for the reality and function of the Holy Spirit being embedded in the mind of the true believer. For this reason, most Christians have at least heard of, if not been taught about God's Spirit, even if it is no more than because of the Great Commission's baptism admonition uttered by Christ in Matthew 28:19. He said, *"Baptizing them in the name of the Father and of the Son and of the Holy Ghost[5]."* Numerous congregations and leaders have taught that He is a Person, but His role as earth's resident Representative of the Godhead remains largely unknown by the wider body of Christ. His Presence in the planet enables the Most High and the Lamb of God to operate what is akin to heaven's embassy on earth through the New Testament ecclesia.

---

[3] Belief in many gods.
[4] Belief in everything as god.
[5] KJV.

Heaven's Embassy

To better make the point, the Holy Spirit in the planet today functions as the Godhead's embassy and Senior Ambassador. On earth, the Holy Spirit is heaven's peacekeeping force sent to see that it does not self-destruct or demonically destruct before the fullness of those to receive Christ's salvation have been born, and born again. He performs for eternity's Sovereign Divine Council every duty, task, detail and responsibility that the ambassadors of the world today perform for their senders. He represents Jesus Christ and the Father God who are creation's joint heads of eternity's new creation nation state, so to speak. In the same way that abusing a political ambassador on earth is dangerous, so is abusing the Holy Spirit, which is why the Lord Jesus says that there is no forgiveness for those who die blaspheming Him.

The Holy Spirit in the World

Within the individual human lives of the world, and the world itself, rejection of the Holy Spirit's forgiveness, salvation, redemption, and embodiment is tantamount to rejecting another state's representative on foreign soil. We all pretty much know how that will turn out. If the head of state recalls its embassy, it means that relations with the abusive state are severed and there is nothing more to expect between two territories but animosity and maybe war. That is the reason why the Lord Jesus gave John the Revelator the Apocalypse that we know today to be the book of Revelation. The entire drama is the Lord's prediction of what will happen to earth for abusing His Spirit and His messengers, rejecting and renouncing His righteousness, and refusing His redemption. Unlike when Jesus restrained Himself from dispatching legions of angels against the earth to prevent His death sentence from Pilate, the Apocalypse tells a very different story. It is consistent with what happens when a sovereign of sovereigns retaliates against a nation that assaults its embassy.

In political terms, such affronts are treated as acts of aggression by the stronger state, and that spells war. When retaliatory war ensues, the weaker nation is destroyed. Such is the case with heaven and earth, the Godhead and the nations of this world. In fact, Revelation 6:14-16 has the earth's world powers begging for the rocks to fall on them to hide them from the face of the Lamb of God sitting on eternity's throne. If you took the time to study ambassadorship, diplomacy, embassies and the like in relation to Jesus Christ's new creation ecclesia, God's everlasting nation-state[6], you would clearly understand two very vital things. You would understand the role and function of the Holy Spirit on earth, and His power and presence in Christ's church. For sure, if you discerned the subliminal comparisons between the two, you would never view the Holy Spirit or the Spirit-filled church of the Lord Jesus Christ the same way again.

The Holy Spirit in the Church

In the church, the Holy Spirit acts as God's immigration agency, the church's bodyguard, and creation's Secretary of State all at

---

[6] Hebrews 12:22-24 and 1 Peter 2:9. To note that Abraham, the old saints, and even Moses understood this, read Hebrews 11, this time from a fresh perspective.

once. He upholds the Lord's celestial government. As the Lord's Immigration Agent, the Holy Spirit certifies who is saved and who is not. Conduct your own study on this subject to grasp what this means to the church of the Lord Jesus Christ and understand God's reasons for establishing the Holy Spirit's regenerative process as the only acceptable means of leaving the ranks of His created beings and becoming His begotten instead. You will learn from your study that what actually makes one a member of Christ's body is the same thing that makes one a naturalized citizen of His eternal nation as well. From your study, you will come to see how the Holy Spirit validates it all according to the Almighty's standard and criteria and not man's. You can get all of this information and insight by studying the following scriptures:

1. Romans 5:5; 8:15-17; 9:8;15:16
2. Ephesians 4: 30
3. Galatians 3:26, 27
4. Philippians 4:3
5. 2 Timothy 1:14; 2:19
6. 1 John 3:1,2
7. Revelation 7:2; 21:27.[7]

The New Birth God's Defining Standard

Different from the nations of this world, one cannot enter God's eternal kingdom apart from the Holy Spirit. A person cannot just put his or her name on heaven's roll and say to the Almighty,

---

[7] As mentioned, on earth the Holy Spirit is definitely heaven's peacekeeping force, sent to see that it does not self-destruct, or demonically destruct before the fullness of those to receive Christ's salvation have been born and born again.

"Now I am your child; treat me like a Christian". That is not how it goes in God's world. In eternal parlance, the redeemed is made so by being born again[8] of the King of Glory[9] – the way all ancient nations were formed. This includes God's lone nation at the time, Israel[10]. The new creature in Christ is royal and the body of Christ His new species' nation, which is what 2 Peter 2:9; 2 Peter 1:3 and Revelation 1:6 all convey.

The Holy Spirit is God's sentinel and border patrol whose job is to prevent illegal entry into the body of Christ, which is what Jesus in John chapter 10 took great pains to explain to us. The Holy Spirit is the eternal kingdom's naturalizer. He naturalizes[11] into Jesus Christ those who wish to live forever as God's offspring[12]. As God's divine agency on earth, the Holy Spirit baptizes God's newcomers into His truth. He is the judge, advocate and divine arbiter who intervenes or intercedes on our behalf. He is the power that separates us from the world, the

---

[8] John 3:6, 8; 8:23; 11:52; 1 Peter 1:23

[9] And in the case of Sarah and Mary, queens (literally princesses)

[10] See Genesis 17 and then Romans 4. Pay particular attention to Romans 4:13.

[11] To admit (adopt) an alien to the rights of a country by a naturalizing process that enables his or her acclimation and adaptation to its government, customs, culture, practices and such as a natural born citizen. To confer upon (an alien) the rights and privileges of a citizen by introducing and converting him or her to a region, establishing and causing the alien to conform and flourish as a native in a land, country, kingdom, etc. To bring into conformity with the nature, environments, and circumstances of a new surrounding after, or in order to grant full citizenship to one of foreign birth to a new place as a native.

[12] See 2 Peter 1:4 that identify the Spirit indwelt that makes the new creature product of the new birth a Christian. In this way, they are made partakers of God's divine nature. The word *nature* includes, to make it clear, a lineal descendent, a genus or sort, a dispositional offspring of a particular lineage, of natural constitution by imparting the very same nature.

signature that signs off on our registry in the Lamb's book of life, and the seal that makes us divine citizens of eternity.

Furthermore, the Holy Spirit is our uplink to the Almighty and His vehicle of download to us. He keeps the channels of communication between Christ and His church open and translates, as any good ambassador does, our communications to the Lord so they are well received. The Spirit of the Lord surveys our individual and ecclesial territories to assure the Redeemer's hedge of protection about us stays secure and that predators do not encroach upon His blood bought church. He further empowers our witness, verifies our testimony, and distributes the provisions and benefits of our New Creation covenant blessings as allocated by the Lord for each of us in Jesus Christ from before the foundation of the world. The Holy Spirit defends us according to God's righteousness and vindicates us when we are falsely accused, or assaulted. In the end, the Holy Spirit will be our transportation out of this world and into the Lord's presence forever. As you can see, the Holy Spirit is the single all-encompassing means of contacting and connecting with God in any way. He is the Godhead's Resident Agent on the planet who interfaces, intercepts, perfects, and permits all of our outreaches to heaven.

The Holy Spirit, God's Skin and Blood

If you are going to enjoy fruitful and vibrant interactions with the Lord, you will need to understand the Holy Spirit of God. To do so, you must comprehend the biological and anatomical structure of the human body above all else because scripture regularly uses it to unlock the mysteries of the Lord Jesus Christ's New Creation church. In preparation for what is to come, I want to call your attention to the scripture passages upon which the following teaching rests, starting with the King James rendering of Romans 12:4, 5. There the Apostle Paul likens the Christian church to a physical body. He uses this comparison to solidify the unity of the diverse members of the Lord Jesus' church, likening each of its member's different functions to the various yet distinct and essential functions of the human body. Paul picks up this vein again in 1 Corinthians 12:12-27, in seeking to validate the church's identity with Christ and the Godhead. To make his point further, he uses the Lord's highest creation, mankind, to insight us on the nature of the Christian church as a result.

Throughout the New Testament, Paul explains how the Godhead—God the Father, God the Son, and God the Holy Spirit—exist as one. They are one because a precise spiritual composition unlike any other, until the incarnation, united them as the same life force. It fused their divine nature into the very same body. This existence in effect describes how they jointly occupy and execute the very same office at the same time: that of creation's Sovereign. It is the same with the biological and physical make-up of Adam's seed. The ecclesia, as its newly engrafted[13] members, is likewise one being formed according to the pattern of the Godhead, creation's first family. Being more like Jesus than any other creature, the church beneath its mortal skin

---

[13] See Romans 11:17, 24; James 1:21.

hides the perfect blend of eternality and deathlessness, flesh and spirit, the human and divine. That is its mystery, and according to Ephesians 3:10, only the principalities and powers in the heavenly places fully grasp it.

To appreciate Christianity's uniqueness requires acceptance of its unrivaled peculiarities. Ephesians 2:16; 4:4,5 and Romans 7:4 all tell us that the church's body is none other than the body of the Lord Jesus Christ that was broken for it on Calvary to distribute itself to those chosen before the foundation of the world to become God's children by Him[14]. Ephesians 5:30 says that Jesus' body is composed of flesh and bones; there is no blood because of what is said in Hebrews 10:16 about His present life source. Christ now lives by the power of an endless life; an indestructible, invincible, deathless life that He passes on to each member of His church upon his or her new birth. The body metaphor used for the Lord's collective descendents is seen throughout scripture and it more than substantiates what I say next.

Who and What is the Holy Spirit?

The Holy Spirit is God's extended self. Scripture calls Him the Spirit of God, the Spirit of the Father, the Spirit of the Lord, the Spirit of Christ, the Spirit of His Son and the Spirit of Jesus Christ. As the Spirit of the Living God, the Holy Spirit's efficiencies characterize Him as:

---

[14] Review 1 Corinthians 12:27 again.

The Holy Spirit's Attributes

Wisdom	Judgment	Burning	Understanding	Counsel
Knowledge	Living	Might	Truth	Holiness
Life	Meekness	Grace	Prophecy	Grace and
				Supplication

Fifteen specific efficacies emanate from God's Spirit that minister to you when you come to God through Him. Some of them treat you before you enter His Presence and others are dispensed to you as a result of coming before the Lord. Combined with the seven personalities given right before them, it is easy to see how all these faculties qualify as the Lord's skin, if you will. What makes skin a good analogy for the Holy Spirit is that skin is considered the largest organ of the body, encompassing its whole outer being. Interestingly, there are three members of the Godhead and there are three differentiated layers to the skin[15]. The Holy Spirit's functional extension as God's skin makes Him what our skin is to our bodies. It performs for Him in like manner. The way our skin completely covers our other two sides, our spirits and souls, as well as our skeleton and vital organs, is in a sense how the Holy Spirit of God covers the Godhead. Think of it this way. Your skin stretches over every part of you as the first

---

[15] The skin is an ever-changing organ that contains many specialized cells and structures. The skin functions as a protective barrier that interfaces with a sometimes-hostile environment. It is also very involved in maintaining the proper temperature for the body to function well. It gathers sensory information from the environment, and plays an active role in the immune system protecting us from disease. Understanding how the skin can function in these many ways starts with understanding the structure of the three layers of skin: the epidermis, dermis, and subcutaneous tissue (Heather Brannon, MD, *Skin Anatomy*, and www.about.com).

point of contact between your invisible self and your world. Among many, many other things, your skin acts like your shield, defense, sensory system, and protective covering at once. That is somewhat how it is with the Holy Spirit. He functions similarly for God in the planet. He shields the unworthy world from God's glory, barricades the Godhead's precious treasures from the devious and destructive, and filters everything that would access the Father. As the Lord's first line protector, the Holy Spirit decides and determines who is who in God's kingdom and ranks each one's access, interaction, and audience with Him. He blocks those who would approach the Lord unlawfully and irreverently. The Holy Spirit covers the Lord's glory, guards Him from whomever He does not want to contact Him, and processes everything before it reaches Him to sanctify and conform it to what our Holy God can enjoy, tolerate, or reject. As incredible as it may sound, this allegory is what the entire New Testament seeks to teach us about our invisible, hallowed, and holy God.

The Holy Spirit knows the Lord in ways no mortal can, because He serves the Father and His Son the way your skin serves you. As the very God Himself, the Holy Spirit tells the Almighty about His creation just as your skin tells you about your world. The way your skin knows you and tells your unseen self about your physical world, God's Spirit constantly informs Him of all that exists and happens in His created worlds in real time. That is what the Apostle John discovered when he said the Spirit witnesses[16] from heaven to earth and earth to heaven[17]. It is also

---

[16] See John 5:22; 8:18; Romans 8:16; 1 John 5:6.

what Paul means when he said that the Spirit bears witness. See 1 Corinthians 2:10-12. In the way your body is notified of agents or elements seeking to infect you, the Holy Spirit similarly reports to the Most High what is approaching or trying to access Him or what should not. Of course the Spirit of God does all of this for Him on an infinitely grander scale.

Before your body is invaded, your skin senses it and begins to alert the rest of you that something is trying to gain access to your inner being. It inspects its nature and decides if it is safe or threatening to you. If there are for instance, certain things that simply do not work for your existence, your skin is probably one of the first parts of you to detect it. If it comes from within, once it reaches the surface your skin shows it to you. Your skin sends signals that announce things to you from within to notify you if they are good or bad, safe and sound or potentially dangerous to you. When something seeks to enter your body, to wage war against it, or wreak havoc with your systems, multiplied billions of sensors on the surface and beneath your skin go into action to investigate, identify, test, approve or prevent it. Your skin's sensors are your feelers, if you will. They raise your defenses or drop your guard usually as a reflex to secure and sustain you. In a similar manner[18], the Holy Spirit does likewise for the Godhead. When it comes to the body of Christ however, the Spirit's surveillance, screening, and shielding activities give us the very same advantages that Christ and the

---

[17] See 1 John 5:7, 8.

[18] After all, scripture does say we are made in the Almighty's image and likeness.

Father have, which is why it is important not to grieve or disregard Him. Study Romans 8:11; 1 Corinthians 11:27; 2 Corinthians 2:10; Ephesians 3:16; 1 Peter 3:18; Hebrews 9:12-10:4, 19, 20; 1Peter 1:2; 1 John 1:7.

The Holy Spirit as God's skin, surprisingly, is found in the Old and New Testaments. In the Old Testament, it is symbolized by the word "tabernacle[19]". The scripture also calls it a tent and covering that equates to skin. See 2 Peter 1:14[20]. Besides this definitions for skin include tent, tabernacle, and covering. For instance, whenever one reads about the Tabernacle of the Lord and its all-embracing coverage of the Godhead's glory housed within it, one is figuratively meeting its skin-like effect. Jesus came and tabernacled among us, as God's skin (see Strong's G4633 and its accompanying string. See also John 1:14 when it says that He dwelt — tabernacled — among us). This means that He embodied the fullness of God within His flesh, which was also considered to be the Almighty's temple (see Strong's 4367[21]). The glory of God manifested in the Old Testament is traditionally expressed as His *Shekhinah,* a word whose original roots liken it to skin. This truth is especially relevant considering Moses'

---

[19] In relation to our skin symbology, the word tabernacle is translated from the common Hebrew for skin, 'ohel.' In this context, it refers to the skin that covered the skeletal structure of Moses' wilderness tabernacle. That is the wooden pillars and such that formed it that were dismantled and enmantled whenever it was traveled or reassembled. The Tabernacle of David, Kevin J. Conner, 1976, KJC Publications, pages 9-11.

[20]Tabernacle there is from Strong's G4638, the word *skenoma,* skay'-no-mah. It means, among other things, the Temple (as God's residence), the body (as a tenement for the soul):--tabernacle.

[21]G463. *skenoo,* skay-no'-o; to dwell or occupy (as a mansion) or to reside as God did in the Tabernacle of old. It is a symbol of protection and communion.

Wilderness tabernacle coverings were actually made of animal skins. They protected what was within, hid it from unworthy and prying eyes, and typified by its three divisions, the three levels of the human body's skin. Allegorically, the tabernacle's badger hide concealed the symbolized Triune God, the tri-part human, and foreshadowed the Son of God's future incarnation. Its divisions were called the outer court, inner court, and holy of holies.

The Skin & the Blood

To continue our comparison between the spiritual body of Christ and your human body, your skin has a very close partner: your blood. Your skin and blood unite to supply a steady stream of life sustaining information about you to the rest of your being. The team also streams all sorts of supplies, nutrients, remedies, recuperative and regenerative powers to you as well. Your skin and blood warn you about dangers, filter and screen what affects your vitality, and communicate what is healthy or harmful to your overall well-being. In effect, your skin is the network that blankets you and your blood is the transmitter that reports on all that pertains to it. Both function as a cohesive intelligence unit that takes care of you, announcing, updating, and alerting every part of your body to what is going on outside of it that may change its insides, and vice versa. Together they take messages from your spirit, your soul, and your organic self and convey them to your outer self, repeating the process from your outer self to notify your soul and spirit of what enters and travels through them to your vital areas.

Here is but a miniscule insight into the importance of the blood of Jesus Christ and its power in the redeemed Christian. It was left on earth to cleanse you from all sin and continually purges you as a member of the body of Christ. It joins the veil (skin) of His flesh via the Holy Spirit to carry out spiritually exactly what their natural counterparts of these functions do for you as a member of His body.

The Holy Spirit, God's Connector

This very, very primitive explanation gives you a sense of how involved the Holy Spirit is in getting you to God and in bonding you with Him. The thing to remember is that the Holy Spirit escorts you into God's presence on His terms and not yours. The Lord decrees how He wants to be approached and what He calls holy, hallowed, sanctified and reverent. These decisions He does not leave up to His worshippers. For instance, in Exodus 3:5, Moses is told by the Lord to remove His shoes because the ground on which he stood before the burning bush was holy. What made it holy? Was it the bush? No. What made that ground holy was the Lord's presence. Moses' shoes classified him as unsanctified, too unsanctified to be addressed by his holy God. The fiery appearance of the Lord to him in the bush was to activate the divine call from His nation's God that drove him into the wilderness forty years earlier. Now the Lord was ready to revive that call and elevate him to priestly and kingly rank by commissioning him, as the God who fathered Israel,[22] to deliver

---

[22] See verse 6 and compare it with Deuteronomy 32:18.

His people from captivity and after that to rule them in His stead. Another example of the Lord's uncompromising holy standard is found later in Exodus 32. It shows how omnipresent and omniscient the Lord's Spirit makes Him. It appears as pervasive as skin on a body. Turn to Exodus 32 with me and read it.

Here is the picture. Moses has ascended up the mount of God to receive the tablets of stone on which the Most High engraved His law, what we now call the Ten Commandments. While Moses is receiving the tablets and the remainder of God's governance directly from His mouth, the people get tired of waiting for him. They grow restless and need to play. Typical of the day, their play involved devilish rituals, revelry and orgies. Moses of course, could not know that any of this was taking place below. He is caught up in the glory of the Lord's presence, but God knows it. His all-seeing Spirit covering the entire multitude has reported back to Him what they are doing. Like skin on His body, the Holy Spirit witnesses and feels Israel's quick and lewd reversion to their Egyptian roots. So after He finishes dictating to Moses, the Lord rushes him back down the mountain to return to his people. Look at what He says and pay attention to how He phrases it below:

> "And the LORD said unto Moses, Go, get thee down; for thy people, which thou broughtest out of the land of Egypt, have corrupted themselves: They have turned aside quickly out of the way which I commanded them: they have made them a molten calf, and have worshipped it, and have sacrificed thereunto, and said, These be thy gods, O Israel, which have brought thee up out of the land of Egypt." Exodus 32:7, 8 KJV

Although Israel's misconduct was unknown to Moses, it did not escape the watchful eye of God's Holy Spirit[23].

Let us go back to the skin analogy again. To summarize, for anything to get into your body, it must pass through your skin. It does not matter if it is a smell through the skin of your nose, sight through your eyes, or a taste in your mouth. Your tissues beneath the surface of the skin are not excluded from this work. To get inside of you everything must start at and go through some part of your skin, and the same is true for anything to get outside of you as well. Over time, all of your senses have learned what is most likely to enter your body based on your environment. In defense of you, it has developed sophisticated instincts that tell it how to admit or prevent any kind of access to you. To make their decisions, your senses instinctually scan and approve, rank and prioritize what to let pass through to you internally and what to ward off to protect you. In these respects, your skin serves as a shield and your blood an intelligence conveyer that briefs your body constantly on what is surrounding and trying to make contact with you. Both imperceptibly guide you on what to receive or reject. Sometimes they leave the response or reaction decisions up to your will; at other times, they make them for you, particularly when hurt or danger is involved.

In every way, your skin and blood are occupied with getting in and throughout you what will do you the greatest good, and halting what will do you harm. Mind you now, nothing in this explanation considers the pleasure pulses that

---

[23] See Isaiah 63:9-13.

your skin must also survey and approve. However, this explains in some ways what the Holy Spirit does for the entire Godhead. He vigilantly and uncompromisingly assures that only what benefits it makes it into the Godhead's presence. The Spirit of God scrupulously keep God the Father and His Son at the greatest advantage and sees that what they want to enter our world from theirs makes it in, as designed and intended, on time.

The Holy Spirit God's Skin

Even though God is Spirit and completely different from the material of our world, it is still safe to identify the Holy Spirit as His skin. Here is why. As said earlier, skin is the human body's largest organ. That makes it all encompassing and pervasive. The Holy Spirit is the largest extension of the Godhead, making Him all encompassing and pervasive throughout creation. The two all encompassing and pervasive fit well with the "omni-everything" terms that characterize God's Spirit. Jeremiah 23:24 has God saying that He fills heaven and earth, while Paul in 1 Corinthians 15:28 states that God Almighty is all in all. With both passages, Ephesians 1:23 agrees. Read the context in which Paul reveals these aspects of God in Ephesians 1:17-23 and 1 Corinthians 15:40. However, more than being celestial, the Holy Spirit, as with the remainder of the Godhead, is uniquely God. What comprises His makeup is not the same as what everything else He made consists of, except for those who are born again in Christ Jesus.

As God, everything abides within the Holy Spirit, and outside of Him nothing exists. Being spread out over all the Lord's realms and territories, since God embodies[24] all of His works, extends the Holy Spirit's housing, protection and surveilling to the Lord's entire visible and invisible, heavenly and earthly worlds. Anything that would make its way to His presence must enter by the veil of His Spirit in the way that whatever would enter you must do so through the veil of your skin. Even though skin can be penetrated, its layered surfaces have numerous defenders to purify it and prevent harm. Similarly, the Holy Spirit's surface can be penetrated, which is why He feels what we do to Him. However, He too has a defense system that, unlike ours, is impervious to destruction. Furthermore, the Holy Spirit is how the Godhead holds at bay whatever it is not ready to receive until it is sanctified and approved by the member of its family that is appointed to discharge this responsibility on its behalf. That is, by the Holy Spirit. Creator God's omniscient, omnipresent skin-like covering performs a host of skin-like tests, acceptance, and rejection duties for the Lord that defend and protect it from our ungodliness, and safeguard and sanctify whatever receives approval to approach it. In this way, He shields the entire Godhead from undesirables and perfectly presents only what the Most High welcomes. In addition, constituting the veil of Christ's flesh that replaced the torn veil of the ancient Levitical Temple ripped by Calvary, God's Spirit carries out for Him and His church everything the Old Testament veils did for Israel and its tabernacle under Moses' Law, and infinitely more. Calling to mind the wilderness tabernacle again to strengthen the skin

---

[24] Refer to Colossians 1:13-22; Ephesians 1:23.

metaphor used for the Holy Spirit, here is how it applies. The largest part of Moses' tabernacle was the outer court. Comparably, the Holy Spirit exemplifies this because as with the tabernacle's skin, He is the largest extension of the Almighty. No one on the planet escapes Him. And, especially since the church's first Pentecost, everyone on earth who wants to come to God must do so by way of His Spirit. The second tabernacle division was the inner court. It is where the Lord's priestly ministrations occurred. This part is reflective of Jesus as the Second Member of the Godhead. We progress to the Most High's presence through the veil of His flesh. Hebrews 8, among other passages ascribe the role of escorting us to God to Him. The most exclusive part of the tabernacle was the holy of holies. It was the holiest of all places on earth. There the Lord's Presence dwelt as tangibly as He could in this world. It held the cherubim shielded ark covered by the gold layered mercy seat that held His law, Aaron's budded rod, and a pot of manna to commemorate His people's wilderness provisions. These all presumably comprised the elements of the very throne of God on earth and the altar that stood before it. But, for our purposes, the Holy Spirit like our skin, housed the most accessible and populated part of the Lord's tabernacle, while the holy of holies its least accessible part. The most sparsely furnished section of the Lord's meeting place held what was most sacred to the Lord. Being a replica of His heavenly ark, the wilderness tabernacle clad with animal skin foretokened the incarnation of His Son in the future. It showed God's people how to worship, honor, and revere the Presence of their awesome God by the

Spirit. Each member of God's family is veiled and protected by the Holy Spirit. And you should know that contrary to popular theology, the Holy Spirit's behaviors and actions in His duties in this respect are neither static nor passive. He is supremely forceful when it comes to protecting His charges, especially when it comes to permitting or preventing what should or should not come near to God.

As the Godhead's number one and most conscientious Guardian, the Holy Spirit becomes warlike when barring anything that wants to enter the Most High's presence from this world if it fails His screening and checkpoints. He resolutely will not present to heaven's throne what is disapproved by God. To block foreign or unapproved entries attempting to bypass Him to get to God the Son and His Father uninvited or disapproved, the Holy Spirit turns aggressive as any high leader's palace, royal, or presidential guard would. Whatever approaches God must remind Him of Jesus and nothing less; Jesus incarnated, crucified, and forever glorified. Rereading Uzza's tragic story in 1 Chronicles 13:9-11 shows how reflexive the Holy Spirit can be when it comes to protecting God's glory and holiness. His behavior in threatening situations spiritually resembles our own skin's defense of our bodies up to and including our muscular reflexes that instinctively act to enable or preserve us. The extreme difference between God's Spirit and us is that the Holy Spirit's invincibility assures nothing that seeks to antagonize or otherwise injure the Godhead penetrates Him, period.

The Holy Spirit and Christ's Church

When it comes to who we are in Christ Jesus, the Holy Spirit's covering and defense expands to the Almighty's most immediate self on the planet, the church, which is the body of Christ. Here, the Spirit of the Lord conscientiously screens all access to it. Sadly, the casualness of His ecclesial authorities often frustrates this safeguard because they are not as discriminating in this regard. Due to compromising indiscretion or naïveté, they stock their churches using a "come one, come all" approach. God's Spirit, on the other hand, stays on task and only opens the gates of Christ's salvation and treasuries to the penitent, despite His earthly ministers' indiscriminate flinging wide the doors of their churches. That sentiment is the essence of Jesus' discourse in John chapter 10 and His declaration of Matthew 16:18.

We the Lord's people should further accept that the Holy Spirit shields the Godhead for His benefit and ours. Before He escorts anyone into its presence, He will examine, thoroughly inspect, and consecrate them inside and out for the visit. At every level before giving audience with Him, God's Spirit will purge, purify, and empower those the Lord receives. Whenever all of the Lord Almighty's reverential requirements are fulfilled, a worshipper or petitioner is then rewarded with nearer and nearer access to the Lord's overwhelming glory, covered by the Lamb's blood to survive it. This principle is practiced just as diligently when the Lord initiates the contact or summons a person He wants to enter His presence. As a case in point, see Exodus 19:11. It is by His Holy Spirit that the Lord purges or adjusts what would enter His presence. According to very specific guidelines and procedures, the Holy Spirit sanctifies and transforms all your overtures and efforts to what the Almighty demands and will respond to most productively. For additional examples, turn to Judges 6:19-21; 13:16-19.

As God's Agent, Sentinel, Shield, and earthly Commissioner, the Holy Spirit has the final say over everything pertaining to the Godhead. That is salvation, healing, ministry, spirituality, decisions of life and death, redemption or damnation; they are all the administrative prerogatives of the Holy Spirit. That is what makes Him God. It does not matter if the preacher, prophet, pastor, or the church itself says otherwise; the Holy Spirit knows God's will concerning all things because He is God. Think about all this in relation to the Lord's church. It is with this impervious incorruptible shield that the Lord Jesus declared that the gates of hell would not prevail against it. God's Spirit is the epitome of meticulousness and as His most trusted earthly Custodian, He allows nothing that belongs to the Lord or that He desires to possess to be diverted from His ownership, use, or control. Whatever the Spirit obtains, He contains; all that the Holy Spirit possesses, He protects; whatever belongs to Christ's body is enveloped by God's Spirit and secured for the Master's good pleasure and sovereignty, and sealed for the day that He returns for His inheritance. Here is what the New Testament scriptures mean about the sealing of the redeemed that the Holy Spirit effects for the Godhead. He is devoted to God, being part of His very self, and will not let anything the Most High obtains or possesses slip through the cracks or be snatched from His fingers. As a indomitable steward over the Lord's purchased possession, the church that He purchased with His own blood, the third Person of the Godhead will not allow anything to be wrenched from His omnipotent grip. He will deliver to heaven's throne what it appointed Him to seek, save, and sanctify at the appointed time.

Also the Godhead is not splintered, fragmented or divided. As scripture says, the Lord our God is one Lord[25] and since the Holy Spirit entwines God the Father and God the Son within Himself, you can see that what they all want is what He delivers for their mutual fulfillment and enjoyment of what they jointly created.

Making Good Spiritual Decisions

Unlike the limits placed on mortal humans, the Holy Spirit actively safeguards the bodies He inhabits and the realms He occupies for the Godhead. Scrupulously, He fields questionable and dangerous effects by blocking or quarantining them until they are rendered acceptable and appeasing to the Most High or verified as disapproved. The Bible calls the objects of His disapproval "reprobate". It is an interesting word that means more than we are commonly taught it does.

I mentioned above Uzza and the wobbly cart that he tried to steady when David was attempting to bring the Ark of God back home as recorded for us in 1 Chronicles 13:7-11. To the

---

[25] Deuteronomy 6:4; Mark 12:29; Galatians 3:20.

unenlightened mind, what happened to Uzza seems harsh and God looks like some sort of picayune invisible assassin who takes pleasure in gathering His people together for sport. First, He moves them to host a celebration in His honor and then at the height of their jubilance He mysteriously lashes out to slaughter one of them unprovoked. However, if you read the entire account with the mind of a priest-king, you will see a whole different side of the incident.

The premise for God's extreme response to Uzza's good intentions stems from His irrevocable charge to His priests. They were to protect His holiness always and never allow any unpriestly person to handle His holy things. David as God's king well knew this and that it was his duty to see that the Lord's priests kept their charge. Moreover, as the nation's monarch he was to see that the priests did their job properly as prescribed by Moses. However, in their exultation over getting God back home, everyone ignored this edict and allowed whoever pressed in to come near and handle the Ark. In addition, having been without the Ark for a long period of time, Israel's Priesthood as God appointed it was defunct. Thus, their instincts and vigilance in this matter were dulled, which made them forget their duty to protect Yahweh's hallowedness. It may have been, from David's words in 1 Chronicles 13:2, 3, that the priests were out of practice and some of the newer ones untrained on how to handle the Ark of God. Whichever it was, God was going to be treated as He desired and not as they imagined.

My recall of this incident, however, goes to God's state of mind on His matters, principles, and precepts. So it deserves deeper study to understand His attitudes and temperament. Here are some points I want you to see about God's will concerning Himself, His possessions and presence. They will show you how His people innately view Him and His order apart from His revelation and the instruction and training of ministers appointed to prepare His people for Him. Below are thirty points on the Uzza incident that may change your perspective of the situation and your view of God as a result.

1. To begin, the Ark of God was captured by the Philistines and held hostage by them for seven months until the Lord decided He wanted to go home to His own land. To gain His own release, He troubled the Philistines with all sorts of plagues to force them to set Him free. See 1 Samuel 6:1-10.

2. After being expelled by the Philistines in order to save themselves, the Ark of God still did not make it home to its appointed resting place for an additional twenty years. Instead, it was waylaid in the home of a resident of a village town in the land.

3. Evidently unbothered by God's absence from their land, the Lord's people went on with life without Him all that time, most of which was when Saul was king. The Ark of the Lord was not in its place when Saul was coroneted. It had been captured and deported by the Philistines when Samuel replaced Eli. All the while Saul sat on the throne, God was held in a single family's home, subject to its will.

4. David sought to bring the Ark back to his capital city because he knew that is where enthroning deities dwell. So he issued the edict to bring the Ark to his capital city Jerusalem, after he seized control of it. He rallied the nation, gathered his national powers and began the task of bringing the Lord home.

5. When the men of Kirjathjearim retrieved the Ark of God from the Philistines twenty years earlier, they immediately set a priest over it to keep the Lord's charge in a feeble effort to comply with Moses' law. Abinadab and His sons who took it into their house at least had the good sense to delegate its attendance to a bona fide priest. Keep this in mind because it is important.

6. The Ark of God abode in Abinadab's house for twenty years. During that time, no one in Israel's capital city or state temple came for it. It was as if, for most of them, out of sight was indeed out of mind.

7. Abinadab's sons were Uzza and Ahio. This is another contributing factor to the Lord's irritation in the incident. While the Ark was in their father's house, they apparently saw it as their family's possession and lost sight of its hallowedness. Nonetheless, they showed some respect for it in that they made touching the Ark the priest's sole responsibility. Its official ministrations were left up to Eleazer the priest, whom they hired to attend to it while it was in their home.

8. When David decided to take the Ark of God to himself, he consulted with his army, political advisors, and the congregation. He had to send for

the priests and Levites because they were scattered throughout the country, being disemployed and banished by Saul. He had slaughtered dozens of the Lord's priests in a violent rage so they went underground in fear of their lives.

9. After gathering the masses, David, on his advisors' counsel, set out to retrieve the Ark of God, presumably in magnificent military style. He was the conquering hero and his armies, particularly his captains assisted him in his consummate kingly endeavor. At last, they were bringing the Ark of their God home to His capital. It does not say where the priests were situated at the time, but the events that unfolded give us a hint; they were not in their God-appointed place.

10. Abinadab's family, who originally rescued the Ark when it returned from the Philistines, brought it out of their house to go home. Uzza, one of Abinadab's sons, drove the cart that they had strapped the Ark to in order to transport it back to the nation's capital. Ahio his brother led the way. (See anything wrong with this picture yet?)

11. As they traveled back home to David's city with the Ark of God, they sang euphorically and played their instruments, celebrating the Lord's return to His capital to be with His anointed king. It was a glorious time, howbeit short-lived. Things were about to turn quite grave very soon.

12. The trip was a long one so they stopped over at Nachon's threshingfloor. As Uzza parked the cart, the oxen carrying the Ark stumbled and threatened to tip it to the ground. Uzza, who had taken care of it for two decades, did what he was

accustomed to doing. He sought to protect it by keeping it from hitting the ground. The problem was that the Ark was no longer in his house, town, or control and the Lord no longer wanted to be handled by him. He wanted to be handled the way He said He wanted to in the Law of Moses: by His anointed priests. Uzza, after such a long lapse of Leviticalism forgot this as did the rest of Israel even David the king.

13. Things had changed; it was a new day that actually returned the nation to its pre-monarchical rules. Freed from His role as a domestic deity petted and petitioned by a single family in a small town, Yahweh was ready to get back into business, God business that is. He wanted to rule from His throne now that He was rescued from Abinadab's living room, so to speak.

14. To steady the cart and keep the Ark from falling, Uzza reached forth his hand to catch it. There should have been no problem with this; after all, he had driven it from Kirjathjearim, his hometown and his father's house. Keeping the Ark of God on its cart of oxen should have been okay since it was in his care for years. By now, he no doubt thought it was his duty as the driver to assure its safe arrival. But it was not, and that mistake cost him his life and David a ton of embarrassing criticism. When Uzza touched the Ark under the new regime, the Lord reacted violently and killed him.

15. Stunned by Uzza's death, David became incensed with the Lord and terrified of approaching Him for a season. He was simply at a loss to explain to his nation what happened to Uzza or say what they

had all done that was so wrong that it caused God to break out against them that way.

16. For the first time since before his inauguration, David and God had a deep rift, and David could not figure out why. Angry with God's behavior, he gave the Lord the silent treatment and refused to bring Him home to His capital city. He left the Ark where it was landed and Obededom came and took it home. God was housebound one more time.

17. David had been so enthusiastic about being made king that he dismissed the importance of God's holiness, even though the archives record God behaving this way before in a similar incidence. See Exodus 4:21-26 and Leviticus 10:1-7.

18. Still smarting from what must have been a painful, mystical object lesson, David decided to let the idea of bringing God home go and abandoned the project. But God was not done with the matter. He still wanted to come home to His capital city and be set upon His own throne.

19. It took David three months to get the message, but finally he did get it. After hearing how the Lord richly blessed Obededom's home while he hosted His presence in the Ark, all Israel was stirred up and probably moved to envy. Word of Obededom's household fortunes got back to the king who also, no doubt, became a little jealous by the news. Seeing all his nation's blessings poured onto one family certainly must have distressed David as king, which was the point the Lord wanted to make all along.

20. Finally, David got the hint and rallied himself and his nation again to bring the Ark of God home

where it belonged, but it seems that in the interim he discovered what went wrong before. The first time he was bringing the Ark of God home to His covenant people the same way it was dismissed by the Philistines from their land, on beasts of burden. That was against the Law of Moses who said that Israel's priests were to carry the Lord on their shoulders.

21. First Chronicles 15:1-4 and 12-15 tell us what happened between God and His king concerning the matter. Here are the lessons David learned as he tried to figure out why the Lord disapproved of coming home with him before the way David chose to transport Him.

    a. David learned that God had a specific way to be transported, and it was not being carted on beasts of burden.

    b. David learned that the Lord had appointed *people* to transport Him: the priests and the Levites anointed to come close to and minister to Him. Here are David's words on the issue that show his understanding of what happened behind the scenes:

> *"Then David said, none ought to carry the Ark of God but the Levites: for them hath the Lord chosen to carry the Ark of God, and to minister unto him for ever."* 1 Chronicles 15:2, KJV

22. David learned that some things were not to be directly handled by him even though he was the king of God's only nation, a principle that cost Saul his throne when he ignored it. When it came to the

Lord and His temple, David was to delegate that responsibility to Yahweh's properly appointed authorities, the Levitical Priests.

23. After learning what he did wrong the first time, David promptly called the head of the priests to handle the detail for him the next time the Ark had to be moved as they should have before when Uzza was killed.

24. By now, David realized that if he had acted differently, Uzza might still be alive. The loss of an innocent life on account of his thoughtlessness as a ruler for sure weighed heavily on the king.

25. Time apparently brought enlightenment and peace to David's mind on Uzza's slaughter and his nation's subsequent judgment. He had failed to reverence the Lord's holiness even if it was confined to that little box. David had permitted God's tolerance for Abinadab's domestic care of the Ark to cause him to lose sight of how the Lord really wanted to be tended to in His homeland. In His official capacity as Israel's God, He still demanded to be regarded as holy.

26. When David was ready to set the Ark of God in the tabernacle that he had specially made for it, he was wiser. He charged Zadok, Abiathar, and the Levites with the duty. He told them to sanctify themselves, something they certainly understood and did so according to God's law in preparation for transporting the Ark of the Lord according to Moses' commands.

27. That David eventually figured it all out is seen in verse 13 where he says to the priests: "*For because ye did it not at the first* (The priests in the first

attempt to retrieve the Ark failed to sanctify themselves and handled the Ark of God personally as was their duty), *the Lord our God made a breach upon us, for that we sought Him not after the due order.*"

28. Because the priests were not the ones handling the Ark of the Covenant when they were bringing it home from Abinadab's house as they should have been, the Lord was displeased about it.

29. The priests understood at this point their part in God's historic rebuke and Uzza's untimely death. They were out of their place, and if they were in place, they were unsanctified. Laxity and irresponsibility led them to permit their duty to be carried out by non-priestly citizens. Therefore, the priests were to share the blame for Uzza's death with David, who failed to remember his obligation to protect and cherish God's glory as His anointed king.

30. At last, the matter could be put to rest. Verse 15 says the priests resumed their duties, positioned themselves and carried the Ark of God properly, on their shoulders, as it should have been at the first. Now God was being treated and transported, as every earthly monarch was to be. He was carried on the shoulders of His temple ministers with no unpriestly hand touching Him, which was just the way He decreed it way back in the wilderness.

Finally, the mystery was solved. Uzza died because he did not recognize the change in God's eras. Once King David and the priests showed up on the scene to retrieve the Ark, Uzza's temporary service was supposed to stop and he was to let them take over the care and defense of God's Presence. However, he did not relinquish his hold on it and they did not assume their duties. The priests, having been furloughed so long by Saul, had probably lost the presence of mind to take over the task of bringing God home on their shoulders. David, a military man at heart, also failed to make the shift. He forsook his obligation to defend God's holiness and forgot that the wooden box held the Presence of the very God that put him in power. That same God had fought beside him helping him win his wars.[26] Now with David firmly seated on the throne, He confined His presence to that little box. Ascending the throne without the Ark of God's Presence and seeing it on a cart pulled by oxen perhaps failed to impress these realities in David's mind, especially since he was but a youth when the Ark was taken, and for a large part of his adult life, Israel's worship of Yahweh did not include it.

In the end, all human parties to the incident acknowledged their part in the matter and admitted that Uzza's shocking death was punitive and indeed the result of their combined dereliction of duty. In admitting their error, they jointly vindicated God's righteousness. He had acted for His own sake, which was His prerogative to do because they failed to reverence Him the way He desired. I could see how God would feel that way considering He had suffered all sorts of indignities as Israel's God for more than two decades; first at the hands of the Philistines when He was forced to reside in the temple with other

---

[26] Psalm 16:8; Psalm 110:1; Acts 2:25.

captured gods. He was installed there because He was considered to be one of their spoils of war and a prisoner because of it. Second, after getting Himself out of that atrocity, He winds up in the home of a citizen instead of being enthroned as the head of state in His nation's capital beside its first king. It is no wonder He was indignant and intolerant. Also, the Lord wanted to make sure that all Israel knew that His return home reinstituted in full the Levitical Priesthood as Moses had appointed it.

An incident such as the one I just recalled would never happen with the Holy Spirit. It was actually His presence in the Ark that defended the Godhead back then. While He was on the cart, the Holy Spirit proved as faithful to Yahweh as ever and swiftly took steps to remind them of how Israel's God was to be treated and transported. As soon as He could assert Himself and make His feelings known, He did so by striking Uzza to make His mind on the situation a matter of public record. If they were going to bring Him home and resume their service and commitment to Him, they were going to start out right. God had been trifled with long enough and He was not about to return to Israel for more of the same. So, He nipped it in the bud by having His Holy Spirit lash out at the entire nation for profaning Him; something that promised, if He did not act for His own sake, to become a way of life for Him. *That*, He refused to suffer any longer.

Guarding the Glory

As guardian of the Almighty's glory, honor, and presence, the Holy Spirit enforces God's boundaries and maintains the lines of communications between God and His people. He is heaven's monitor and the transmissions link with earth and vice versa. Unfortunately, most Christians do not acknowledge this standard of God's. They dismiss any idea of His having an all-pervasive side that protects Him or that it extends from His world to ours. Those who do so cannot imagine how exalted the Creator's technology is in comparison to earth's and fail to see any need for it. Therefore they also fail to appreciate the Holy Spirit's function of screening their access to God. Many Christians furthermore live unaware of the Holy Spirit's role in their salvation, sanctification, and spiritual life. They cannot conceive of the Holy Spirit as God and certainly cannot fathom what the big deal is about Him. As far as some Christians are concerned, He is useful for speaking in other tongues and maybe a few other antics some zealous branches of the church like to engage in to show off. But for the most part, those who do not wish to speak in tongues or to get too deep in God prefer to ignore Him. In return for their attitude, many of them get the silent treatment from the Lord. When you wish to commune with your Lord, remember the Holy Spirit is the only way you will get through to God the Father and your Savior Jesus Christ. Also, remember that He has a duty to them both to prepare you to be received with grace and favor. For these reasons, make it a point to learn about God's Spirit and press to understand how vital He is to fertile interactions with the Father and His Son. Submit to His work in your life so your times with each other are mutually satisfying and rewarding. If you want glorious times in God's presence, do not presume upon or grieve

His Spirit as He alone is the way that happens. Realize that He presents us to God according to His criteria and not our sentiments or sincerest intents.

No matter how brief your encounter with the King of glory is to be, God's Spirit is in you and in the world to see that only the best gets through to Him and comes out of every moment you spend together. The model standard for that best, by the way, is none other than Jesus Christ. Diligently and vigilantly, God's Spirit keeps the Lord in touch with His creation and His creation in touch with its Sovereign Creator. Therefore, in the same way that you are useless without your skin and all of its layers and thus vulnerable to everything the world can throw at you, so are your attempts to commune with God vain without the Holy Spirit. You need your skin and all its manifestations to make you presentable, functional, sensitive, and safe. It is indispensable for healthy contact with your world. When it comes to your celestial self and your interactions with the eternal God, you need God's skin, the Holy Spirit, for the very same reasons. Jesus reiterated this time and again in preparing His disciples for His departure. He sought to allay their grief over His leaving by letting them know that He would return to them in another form, in the form of a Comforter (Helper or Paracletos) who would be with them and within them to assure they enjoyed unhindered access to Him and our heavenly Father. That Comforter the Lord introduced as the Holy Spirit, whom He would dispatch from heaven once He returned home. Without the Holy Spirit, you cannot even get a message to the Lord, which is why it was so important to the Father to dispatch Him into the world to indwell His church.

Chapter Three

Hollow vs. Hallowed God Contact

David begged God once, according to Psalm 51:11, not to take His Holy Spirit from him. What kind of relationship must they have enjoyed that made the king beg the Lord not to do such a thing? What was it about their times together that made the thought of God no longer intimately talking and walking with him a terrifying prospect? What caused David to plead for God's company more than anything else in his entire realm? Psalm 42:1 gives us a clue. It says that David panted for the Lord God more than anything else he did. In comparison to the vulgar Christianity of today, what David discovered about being with his God appears to have been more than the popular "Jesus is my personal Savior who understands me and accepts me the way I am" type of relationship. Such pathetic redemption goes hand in hand with the type of salvation that brags, "Christ died to free me to do and be whatever I choose." As prevalent as that attitude is today among the so-called modern liberated Christians, it is nonetheless an unsaved one that comes from not knowing or truly experiencing the God-Man Jesus Christ at all. Such relations merely force one's will upon the idea of a savior with no intention of ever submitting to one.

Another perspective on God that is popular today comes from the "I'm searching to find out which god is the best pick for me" mentality that keeps the seeker forever on hunting for the best god to serve, and all deities at the mercy of his or her religious whims. That type of faith is just talk. It is more in love with the *quest* for a god than with making any connection with one. It just wants to get high off of the next spiritual encounter and sample new ones whenever the fervor over the last one gets stale. It is the people's religion, the "me, myself, and I" religion that cannot bear being too close to the real Lord. Such childishness and insensitivity delights in stretching the limits and pushing the envelope. Taking risks with their salvation is fun to them because all they have to bring to the Lord's altar is their immaturity and selfishness anyway. Being duty bound to Jesus for them is out of the question. These souls have no problem binding the Lord to His duty to them and shirking theirs to Him at the same time. Not so with those who truly ache to be one with God in His presence.

When God Goes Silent

God's sincere seekers long to go way beyond just being saved members of His body. They literally strive to become as He is in their world, to be of a like mind and of the same spirit with Christ in every way. For them, a simple misstep or error in judgment is distressing, not because they fear going to hell, but because they genuinely care about their Lord and what affects Him. These people have a deep concern for what happens between them and God. They need to discover and experience everything that takes place between them and the Lord firsthand. Sincere worshippers do not think, "I'll just take it by faith that God hears me and everything is working okay between us. I know He cares for me, even if years go by without me ever hearing from Him." Presumptuous worshippers believe that how they approach God is how He should be approached, and how they choose to relate to Him is how He should be treated. Sincere worshippers are thoughtful folks. To them God is a Person, a real Person, with feelings, needs, and experiences of His own. Somehow, deep within they sense, and as a result behave, as if there is much more to the Lord than they can see or meet at first. Perceptively, they recognize that God has lived through, endured, and overcome a lot more than He can ever reveal to any of us. Instinctually, they sense that all He has lived through makes Him all that He is as the Almighty in the same way our experiences make us who we are in this world as His creatures.

True worshippers want the best for God as much as He wants what is best for them, so they do all they can to keep the lines of communication between them open and their intimacy robust. To these people a relationship with God is not a one-sided mystical experience. They want to shoulder their load and live up to their responsibility to the Lord as much as they expect Him to do the same for them. These people also do not want their connection with Him to be confined to life in this world. Genuine worshippers know that God too has visions, hopes, desires, and dreams that began before humans were made and they want their daily fellowship with Him to fulfill the reason He created them. As a result, offending the Lord in their mind is not only irreverent, it is unthinkable because it threatens to interrupt their constant and comforting companionship with God, what they prize above all else. There are millions of people like this on the planet today. If you are still reading this book, you are probably one of them, or called to become that type of a Christian.

Frankly, as hard as it is to believe because of society's wide scale irreverence, the Lord is more popular than you or I are led by mainstream media, humanist educators, and stagnant religionists to believe. The Holy Spirit has been extraordinarily effective in publishing and promoting the Almighty and Jesus Christ worldwide generation after generation, and they still have quite a hold on their world. Those who would have you think otherwise are either angry with God or disagree with His way of life. To justify their peeves and conflicts with Him, really more accurately His church, they spew streams of nonsense aimed at disproving His existence or ridiculing faith in Him. Such vendettas bank on your personal insecurities to foster an inferiority complex in you about your hunger for the true and living God that will bully you into disowning Him as well. Their blasphemies dare you to confess the name of Jesus or to express your love for Him as your Savior, especially publicly. These people are bent on intimidate you into willful surrendering to their demonically inspired campaigns against the true and living God. Talking to or hearing from the real Jesus Christ is not their desire, which would almost be okay if they did not want to keep you from talking to or hearing from Him, too.

If you left it to the publicity mongers of our time, you would think the last thing *anyone* on earth wants is to know God, whom they erroneously confuse with religion. They would have you to believe that understanding Him enough to become close to Him is unsophisticated and only for the poor and destitute. Do not buy the hype. Not everyone on the planet is a vengeful Catholic school brat angry with the religious people who reared them, or a vengeful preacher's kid resentful a parent's devotion to God or His ministry. Many such attitudes stem from childish jealousy of a family's love for God and devotion of their homes and families to His righteousness and holiness. And then there is the one who as a youngster grew up in the hyper-carnal church who cannot fathom that maybe where he or she went to church just was not at all serious about the Lord. These people take their lone experience as an excuse to ridicule God altogether because they cannot imagine that there are churches and Christians out there that are quite faithful to Him. Contrary to libertine Christian claims, the world is still full of people who love the Most High God and the Lord Jesus, and they love them just the way they revealed themselves to the world. They do not want to change either one of them or modernize them, if you will. You may be just one of those people; one of those who crave God's company and yearns for His presence. You may be one who delights in His personality and enjoys Him as the holy God He is. You do not need to downplay or misrepresent Him to make Him more palatable to your spiritual appetite. You perhaps feel the Lord is compatible with you and work to be as compatible with Him. You do not care if He is stylish to your friends. If any of these is you, then your affection for Jesus and your communion with Him are unquestionably hallowed and not hollow. You love and delight in the Lord as He is with no vain imagination to excuse your humanity.

Really Knowing Jesus is to Fall Deeply In Love with Him

Many people say they love God and want more of Jesus. Thousands of sincere Christians pray every day for the Lord to commune with them in a fuller and more gratifying way. They beg God to touch their spirits and fill their lives. Sadly, though, if you spoke with them at length, most of the people who do so demand that God respond to them on their terms. It does not matter if those terms are according to their religion, theology, doctrine, favorite preacher, or cherished romantic notions about what being close and faithful to the Lord really is. Unless He bends to most people's will, God can forget any meaningful relationship with them. So, He simply stays silent, working quietly in the background to bring about His will in their lives. That is the source of God's silent treatment with most souls. It goes back to the Uzza incident for Him. The true and living God is particular about how He wants to be served. Communion and fellowship with our Heavenly Father do not rest on human preconditions as most people think, but on His preferences and needs. For many worshippers these are the least important. This is because many people, even believers, have deep-rooted issues with the very essence of who God is and what He stands for that reinforces the barrier between them. Others are experiencing those same barriers because they were taught the Lord by people who had difficulty with Him. And then there are those who are convinced that God's righteousness is impossible and sin in comparison is easier, or more fun. Those fitting either category are the worshippers who will negotiate the terms of their relationship with the Lord as a condition of their faithfulness. Their prayers go something like this: "If you do this first Lord, then I will do that; as long as you do such and such Lord, I will do such and such; but now that you have ceased to do this and that Lord, I cannot or will no longer do thus and what." Their prayers, worship, devotions, and sacrifices to God all have rigid one-sided strings attached to them that bind the Lord and yet frees them from His standards. The moment the Lord fails to deliver on the reason they chose Him to be their God in the first place, they get angry and begin to punish Him. His punishment usually starts with pouting. After this, God gets the silent treatment—they stop seeking Him or praying. From here things escalate as they begin to break their promises to Him. Over time, they discontinue communing with Him, skip church, and resign from their ministry positions to ignore Him.

The granddaddy of all the ways God's children punish Him is with the only real power they feel they have, their money. When God disappoints some people, they retaliate with monetary stinginess. In their ire, resentment, or disappointment, these folks stop tithing, sneer at offerings, or insult the Lord by giving Him pennies on the dollar for not doing things their way. They cease to regard Him or tolerate anything related to God. Over time, they grow sullen, surly, and critical of everything church and Christian. Somehow, these people think their vengeful behavior hurts the Lord more than it does them. While it does affect God, in the end it hurts them infinitely more, and costs more than they ever wanted to pay in the way of life disruptions and unnecessary losses. Thankfully, that scenario does not describe all of God's saints.

Christ has countless people who see their communion and fellowship with Him as a top priority. They rejoice in building and continually strengthening a true and living bond with the Savior and see it as their lifeline. These souls do not find the Lord's word, works, and worship weighty and oppressive. For numerous worshippers, it is the extreme opposite. For them the, the thought of losing any ground with the Most High at all strikes terror in their hearts. They dread the wall of silence that will go up between them, knowing it can last days, months, or years depending upon the seriousness of their tension. These are not the irrational fanatics that one might imagine. Many of these people are bright, intelligent and successful in life, outside of their unshakeable faith in their God. Yet, they have managed to break the seal on relations with the Almighty that much of the world does not even know exists. And, do not think that you can spot them by sight, because they are everyday people whose real differences show up in their prayer closet when the rest of the world is shoved out. Those who have met with God behind the veil by way of the Holy Spirit, and not according to the dictates of the church, are deeply in love with their Lord and vow inwardly never to let anything negative happen to their relationship with Him. They do not share the worldly saint's problem with conforming to His character and conduct in life. These people dread offending or distancing themselves from God because they have formed, and desire to maintain, a unique implacable and irreplaceable bond with their Maker. If it is broken, they know it will leave a deep chasm in their soul, a vacuum that nothing else in this world can fill. If you have ever had that happen between you and God, you know that it is a lonely, haunting experience that you would never want to relive. That is because you have feasted on the Lord in ways carnal Christians cannot imagine, and you do not take lightly any type of silence from Him. Were He to stop responding to you, it would not take days or years for you to realize that He has gone silent in your life. You are the person I am writing to because, like David, you pant after the Lord and crave your times of communion and your special place with Him. You do not find hallowedness drudgery, and you do not feel ridiculous reaching out to Him even though only your spirit and heart can see, feel, or touch Him. The Spirit of God within you has erased all the barriers that blind you to His existence and mute your ears to His voice.

As a worshipper of the true and living God, you cherish what you share with your heavenly Father and because the Holy Spirit is intimately involved in your entering and enjoying His presence, He easily makes God tangible to you. You are a sincere worshipper who depends on your precious moments with God. Actually, it could be said that you are addicted to them because they reward you with so much more than can never be put into words, no matter how many journals you fill. Those closest to you discern this about you and the Lord, and unfortunately some of them want to label you as fanatical because they feel shut out of what happens between you two. That is how it should be when love is real. Parties in love cherish what they have and do all they can to guard what they share. That reality should not change just because the number one love of your life is your Lord. If He is, then you are unique, one of a fragmentary few in comparison to all the souls alive today. Every time you enter the Lord's presence, it is a wonderful and glorious excursion that you cannot wait to relive again and again and again. For you, Hebrews 11:6 is a continual reality. You come to God freely and enthusiastically because you know that indeed He is, and you have discovered that He truly is "a *rewarder* of those that diligently seek Him." For you God's silence is not a relief from unpleasant religious chores or an escape from an austere deity. It is a sign that something is amiss between you that you want to straighten out as quickly as you can.

Because you are who you are to the Lord, and because of the fervent devotions you enjoy, you know something about Him that only living in His presence and roaming around in His soul can reveal; something that you are not about to risk on anything. While there may be a prized few of us who feel this way in comparison to the multitude of those professing Jesus Christ, we are indeed precious and delightful to Him. When God grows silent with us, it is terrifying, confusing, and utterly crippling to our life-walk. Yet sometimes the Lord does go silent on us without telling us why at the outset. Hopefully, if you have lived through it, or are wrestling with this side of Him now, the wisdom in this book will help you reopen or keep the heavens open over your union with God and the channel of communications between you unfettered by the nonsense of this world.

What Sets You Apart as a Worshipper

Open heaven communications saints experience something with the Lord that makes them feel safe, secure, and desirable to Him. Their intimacy makes these saints feel uniquely covered by His love and protected. Holiness and sanctification do not frighten these people away from His intimacy. In fact, it is the other way around with them. It grabs them. Their times with God drive them to return to Him time and again on their own. An open heart and soul enriched by true faith gives the Most High complete freedom to be Himself as God and Lord. When they enter and leave His Presence, they are empowered and more fruitful in life. Releasing God's Spirit to inject His wisdom and counsel into their decisions comes easy because they do not live to resist or evade Him. True worshippers value His intervention in their lives and commit to cooperating with Him fully if for no other reason than that He has been around and successful for ages. This is aside from His having saved their souls. For hungry worshippers, obliging God's sovereignty is not the compulsory motive for seeking Him; love, compatibility, and paternity are what compel them. God is their Father in truth and not just in concept. They cling[27] to God because years of ardent fellowship, time and patience taught them how delightful He really is. For these souls, simultaneity with God takes precedence over passive attachment to Him. Simultaneity[28] is oneness, plus intimacy, plus synchronicity, plus synergy, plus passion. By definition, *simultaneity* means precisely performing on earth what is being done simultaneously, at the very same time, in heaven.

Encounters with the Almighty of this type are not the overly *carnalized* fantastical illusions pushed on us by an indifferent church. You know the sort. It is the communion that deals with the Lord without all the fuss of sanctification, conformance, and transformation. The kind of communion that believes sanctification and holiness are strictly God's responsibility; the worshipper just comes as they are to get what

---

[27] Deuteronomy 4:4; 10:20, 22; 13:4; 30:20; Joshua 22:5; 23:8; Jeremiah 13:11; Acts 23:11.
[28] See Matthew 6:10; 1 John 3:3, 7; 4:17; Mark 16:20.

they can. These people feel out of place in the deep things of God and woefully out of their league with His Spirit. The only way they can relate to the Lord of glory is to bring Him down to their level and downplay His hallowedness. Such a relationship with the Lord just has to stylize the Almighty and Jesus Christ for modern times. It just has to overly humanize Him to make Him more enjoyable and less discomforting to earthly mortals. To such saints, the deep things of their Christian walk should be put off until later in their salvation, perhaps just before Jesus comes or just before they depart this earth. Until then, the goal is to use God as they see fit and oblige Him to serve His creaturehood as it desires, and dodge everything else about Him that puts pressure on their spirituality.

Being the longsuffering Father that He is, the Lord appears to put up with such treatment because He knows the end of these lives[29]. He knows that the tables will turn soon enough on those who dismissed Him so casually in the beginning of their lives. Before long, reality will set in and force them to return to Him when they find out that there is no comparable alternative to Him as their God. When the replacement gods that people choose prove to be as powerless and impoverished as the Most High knows them to be, better yet bankrupted them to be, they will have to return to the true and living God for help and recovery. Sometimes this leads them to repentance and faith in Jesus Christ and at other times, it just makes them bitter or determined to

---

[29] See Psalm 2:4.

bargain with God all the more to continue having their way with Him.

To those like you and me on the other hand, who pant after the Lord the way King David did, intimacy means something more. It is not a buzzword but a real entwinement with your Heavenly Father. You see and crave your relations with the Lord to mirror the very same exalted intimacy that Jesus through the Holy Spirit had with Him as His heavenly Father on earth. For some of you out there, nothing less will do. The intimacy you value is where Christ, in His human form and His earthly ministry, and His Father constantly lived as indivisibly one. They abode in a place of mutual regard and delight that caused neither one to presume upon the other ever, which is how, according to John 10:28, they remained inseparably one in every way. Neither God the Father or the Son Jesus Christ permitted anything to put even the slightest distance between them. Protecting what they shared was more than an ideal that they pursued; it was a nonnegotiable necessity if they were going to remain in power over the worlds they had made. If any of this speaks to you, you undoubtedly perceive the matchlessness of their intimacy and desire a measure of it for yourself. You live impressed with how pure the Godhead's union remained when Jesus walked the earth, and can easily take it as a model. You discern and revere their mutual admiration for each other and cherish what each one thought, celebrated, and prized about the other. That intimacy is what made Jesus gladly subject Himself to His Father's will and desire to please Him all the way up to the cross. He could withstand the trials He faced and ultimately endure the horrors of Calvary because He enjoyed an uninterrupted and unlimited communion with His Father in heaven that far outstripped the rival temptations of this world. God in turn rewarded Jesus with an open heaven, as John 1:51 shows that far exceeded what He did for Jacob in Genesis 28:12. Whereas Jacob's ladder bestowed heaven's blessing *upon* Jacob, Jesus Himself, when the heavens were opened to Him, was made the actual ladder itself. John's gospel says that God the Father gave the Son of Man the Holy Spirit without measure.

How True is Your Intimacy with God?

True intimacy with God the Father, like that practiced by Jesus Christ, responds to and is rewarded with a true revelation of Him and His Father. See John 14:21-23. That intimacy does not seek to dismiss the holiness of their Godhood or their joint authority as the Godhead. Instead, it takes a real delight and confidence in both. True involvement with God at the deepest level makes you faithful, loyal, determined and resolved. It gives no place to estrangement and does not crave the easy way out. Rich communion with the Lord is not the paganistic ritualism that some are peddling today. It is also not based on the individuality of two people claiming to be in love who have no intention of truly giving themselves to each other or surrendering anything to or for their relationship. One does not seek God for a religious arrangement because he or she knows that the Lord never responds to His people out of sheer religion. The beauty of His love does not seek purely sensuous outcomes for gratification. God leaves that to the flesh, which is why Jesus stated in John 4:23 and 24 that to worship the true and living God, one must do so in spirit and in truth because that is what the Father is seeking. Jesus' open communications intimacy with His Father in heaven were not like what much of the modern church endorses at all. What our Lord demonstrated for, and offers to, us He envisions for the church. His brand of intimacy is His greatest desire and gift to us. At its least, it requires us to cease being ourselves and to become in His presence wholly what and all that He is. When it grows and matures, such worship becomes reverently comfortable with the Lord and respects God for all that He is and presses to please Him in every way. Pure intimacy produces strong relations with the Lamb and fuels a profound regard for His glory and holiness. It refuses or overcomes the temptation to belittle God's reverence and sweetly reminds us of how and why we will never be totally equal to Him. Both revelations are comforting.

Jesus Christ, how we come to and worship God is holy, eternal, and "omni-everything." Look at what Hebrews 7:26 says about Him: *"For such a High Priest became us, who is holy, harmless, undefiled, separate from sinners, and made higher than the heavens"* (KJV). No amount of earthly achievements, acquisition, or endowments can come anywhere near what our God is and has made of Himself or us. For all of these reasons, endeavoring to partake of God's greatness and goodness, His warmth and fellowship demands doing things His way. That means you must conform your perceptions, attitudes, and overtures toward Him to Leviticus 10:3, what Peter reiterates in 1 Peter 1:15. Here is what the Leviticus 10:3 passage says, *"Then Moses said unto Aaron, This is it that the Lord spake, saying, I will be sanctified in them that come nigh me, and before all the people I will be glorified. And Aaron held his peace."* Peter adds, *"But as he which hath called you is holy, so be ye holy in all manner of conversation; because it is written, be ye holy; for I am holy."* The Bible says that without holiness no one shall see the Lord. This is a take off of Jesus' Beatitudes where He said, *"the pure in heart shall see God."* You cannot connive your way into God's presence or heart. You also cannot pick Him up and put Him down as you feel like it. Here is a word to the wise. Irreverence will court His displeasure and then nothing good can happen between you and the Lord. The only thing you end up doing is silencing His voice to you. Do not ever risk it. Make every effort in your walk with Christ never to shut down communications between you and Him. No matter how deep your wounds, broken your heart, or painful your trial, resolve never to cut off your communications with God. Ride out the difficult times; stay faithful and prayerful during them. Somehow, things will begin to make sense to you again in time. As you ride them out, do everything to keep the door and channels between you and the Savior open and your communion fresh and vibrant. In fact, at such times, boost your times with the Lord; do not slack up on them. I say this because when God goes silent, so does everything else of substance about Him, and it can take years for you to convince Him to resume communications with you. The chapters to come tell you why you want to keep the channels of communication open between you and God, how not to silence Him, and what to do if it ever happens to you.

Chapter Four
The Shock of God's Sudden Silence

There is no greater suffering a saint of God can live through than God's sudden silence. Its affects are doubly painful if it happens to a genuine prophet. The vacuum of deafening silence it creates within can be traumatically worse when a prophetic communicator ceases to hear from God. When months or years, and if the cause is serious enough, decades go by without the Lord opening His mouth to a prophet that He once vigorously communed with nonstop, it is crushing to say the least. A chilly tremor runs through your spine when you suddenly wake up one day and realize that it has been weeks, months, or maybe years since the Lord said anything to you, particularly anything prophetic. God going silent on a prophet means it has been a long time since He sent a prophetic dream or transmitted a highly predictive vision, unveiled a revelation, or even answered a question. Prayer becomes empty and stagnant, worship and devotions merely perfunctory. Prophetic words usually given to the messenger in His name are halted as night upon night passes without any vision from the Lord, as Micah 3:5-7 puts it. Knowing what is going on in the future by the Lord's hand now becomes as impossible for the once fertile prophet as it is for those seeking the Lord's word from the messenger's mouth. These become very dismal times for fervent prophets, and they can drag on forever.

Once the Lord determines that He no longer wants to share His deep secrets with a certain prophet, the minister's life takes an ominous turn. Whether or not speaking engagements cease or wane, the messenger inwardly experiences a void that God's silence suddenly created within. In these instances, fear grips you every time you have to speak, especially when you have to prophesy. Others expect you to prophesy, but you know you will have to make it up because God's not talking means that anything you say will come out of your own spirit and not from the Lord. See chapter Ezekiel 13:1-16 for eighteen signs of the Lord going silent on a particular messenger. He or she:

1. Is forced to prophesy out of their own heart.
2. Is forced to follow their own spirit.
3. Sees nothing.
4. Fails to build a hedge about god's people.
5. Envisions futility.
6. Resorts to false divination.
7. Travels about ministerially without being sent by God.
8. Prophesies hopeless prophecies hoping they will come to pass.

9. Declares "thus says the lord" when he has not spoken to them.
10. Declares false visions and lies.
11. Claims and envisions nonsense and lies.
12. Seduces God's people with cries of peace in blatantly troubled times.
13. Shut out of God's prophetic council.
14. Looses the prophet's place in His registry.
15. Lead God's people to stray from Him.
16. Builds feeble hedges that cannot hold in difficult times.
17. Weakens God's hold on His people and their hedge of protection.
18. Subjects the Lord's people to His just judgment.

All of these consequences can go unnoticed by the typical believer following a particular prophet's ministry until it is too late. You however do not have to wait until then. You can just evaluate the questionable messengers in your world according to the above list and realize what the problem is. If more than a third of the above have become commonplace in the person's ministry then, you can probably safely conclude that the Lord has gone silent on that voice and Deuteronomy 13:3 is perhaps a good response for you as a result because the Lord is signaling that He no longer trusts that messenger to bear or deliver His word in truth.

If you are a true prophet and this is happening to you, it will seem as if it were better for you to have never heard the Lord's voice in the first place than to have it abruptly stop. Again and again, you ask yourself, what if others find out you are faking it because you are prophetically dry and out of communion with God?

The possibility of being found out only compounds the situation for you. Things are dreary within and bleak outside as you keep up appearances, plodding along as if nothing has changed, hoping the answers and the words you give do not shipwreck those with whom you are pretending. That is, if you are genuinely concerned about God's people.

Take Care of Your Communion with God Now

For these reasons, you should take care of and value your interrelations with the Lord now. Avoid trivializing what is important to Him. Do not get so comfortable with God's presence and overtures that you fail to recognize that He too has boundaries. Although His patience is longsuffering, there are behaviors the Lord simply will not tolerate from anyone, particularly from His prophets. When thoughtless or headstrong messengers persist in them and they take their toll on God's souls, lives, and adversely affect His credibility, He will turn the light off. Your dream life and spiritual sight will cease as the God of your prophetics refuses to speak to or through you as His messenger again. Sometimes this can last a few weeks or months and at other times, it can be permanent, as it was with Saul who so disappointed the Lord that he caused Him to withdraw His Spirit from His brand-new king. Despite what free-wheeling believers may say, God does have His limits and when you transgress them, He may go silent without ever telling you why. To prevent this from happening to you, you should know the things that can silence the Lord's voice to you prophetically or otherwise and avoid them. That way you can forestall such a devastating event in your own relationship with God Most High.

When God Does Go Silent

When the Lord stops responding to a prophet's devotions or conspicuously ceases to answer prayers, it is a serious matter. His doing so can signal His displeasure or concern over misconduct, indifference, or offense. On the other hand, sometimes God's silence can simply mean you need to get ready to shift gears and take your ministry in another direction. When this is the case, it is wise to take time out to seek His mind and will for what to do next. Usually before He goes silent on you for any reason, He will send you a few other prophetic voices to inform you of His intent. If you dismissed their words, God's doing what He prophesied can take you by surprise. When you run into trouble for ignoring Him, He may choose to ignore your inquiries or petitions in response for a season.

When other issues are the cause for God's silence, stubbornly staying the course may not be the wisest thing for you to do. It may be more prudent for you to take yourself off the scene voluntarily to figure out what is provoking Him to close off your communications, and the sooner you do so the better. If you take the initiative, things may be able to return to normal rather quickly. If not, there can be a protracted contest between you and the Spirit of God that robs you greatly of His customary rewards for faithful service.

In either case, when God stops communicating, it is because He wants to get your attention and His ordinary attempts at doing so have failed. To snap a person's consciousness awake to His need to address some issues between them, the Lord will simply close off His revelatory streams. It is then that the messenger learns that all the splash and dash he or she previously enjoyed were really the handiwork of the Almighty after all. Shutting off a believer's ability to hear His voice or to understand what He is saying, or means by what He says, is the most effective way to get a minister's attention, prophetic or not. Whatever God's reasons or methods for doing such a thing, seasoned servants know their signs well. Years of waxing and waning with God have taught them not to dismiss His initiatives under such circumstances. Sharp rebukes and stern object lessons have taught veteran ministers to read the signs of God's summonses well. Even still, some of them dismiss or dread them.

In these instances, God's tug on our attention is the same as with any employer and employee relationship. When your boss calls you into a meeting, you naturally get a little anxious. On a secular job, you cannot skip the meeting without risking your position. With God's messengers however it is different. They tend to take excessive liberties with His summons and refuse to meet with Him on a matter. Many of them for any number of reasons drag it out for years sometimes until the Lord must resort to the sternest measures to get them into His presence to discuss His issues with them. Knowing this lackadaisical trait of His ministers is why His notices to some of them to meet with Him on occasion have to be so strict. It is also why His summons to them to address the gravest situations often starts out stern and will turn harsh if He is continually disobeyed. If a messenger or minister instinctually knows what the Lord wants to talk about, like David who took three years and a famine to make His way to Yahweh's throne on the Bathsheba issue, he or she will use a variety of stall tactics. From being too busy on the road to feigning an inability to hear or understand God clearly anymore, the evasive tactics can delay the inevitable for years. This is unfortunate since in the end it only hurts the minister and his or her ministry when the Lord has to bring down a heavy hand on the situation to compel obedience to Him.

The thought of the Lord abruptly beginning to ignore one of His children after years of rich and gratifying fellowship is grieving. When it happens to a prophet, it fills the devoted messenger with great, though often unspeakable, terror. The prophet begins to wonder if he or she is receiving a supernatural "pink slip" from the King of kings or being readied for promotion. Both or either can be the case. The upside is that if the prophet has not allowed the situation to go on too long, he or she will begin to seek the Lord, and search recent behaviors and attitudes to discover the problem, if there is one. Frequently, not long after the messenger identifies what went wrong, the Lord will voice His feelings and things get back on track.

Unfortunately, God's goodness has the tendency to lull indulgent, presumptuous, or dull-hearted messengers into such contentment that by the time they realize things have changed between them, much damage has been done. Years of shrugging off God's unction and dismissing His efforts to communicate outside of the comfortable, professional, or profitable only make the situation worse. After too much time passes, the prophet becomes at a loss as to where to begin to sort out the matter. When this happens, it is not just God who goes silent, but it is His spiritual forces as well.

God's Silence Also Silence His Spiritual Forces

Prophets' intimacy with the Lord involves a vivacious spiritual life that engages His heavenly forces as well as the Lord Himself. His abrupt shutdown of His communications is reinforced with their shutdown as well. A sudden awareness of the absence of God's assigned angelic guard and their customary activity or attention normally given to the prophet to empower the ministry is poignantly felt. Their sudden inactivity adds to the prophets' grief because instinctually they know why. Inwardly, prophets above all sense that when the Lord instructs His supernatural agencies to withhold their support and to draw back their hands from them, it further solidifies the breach between them (see Mark 8:38 and Luke 9:26). The most tragic and extreme illustration of this in scripture is found in Ezekiel chapter 9. It shows when happens when God becomes estranged from His people. Harsh and deadly things happen that He seems indifferent to and refuses to intervene to help. Prayer does not work and like Saul, nothing seems to placate Him. This for a prophet is a terrible place to be that should be avoided at all costs. Because, to feel secure and affirmed by his or her God, every devoted messenger needs the channel of communications to stay open and the stream of spiritual support that established and maintains the ministry's potency to remain intact. For a good scripture example of how the angels and agencies of God function in the arrangement, turn with me to Joshua 5:13-15. Let us go over it together.

Joshua, Moses' successor, was the Lord's military prophet. Moses' military might and national leadership were passed onto him upon his predecessor's demise. At this point in Joshua's new service to Israel's God, he is brought into the secret of Moses' staggering success. It is a military angel assigned to undergird his physical efforts. That, Joshua learned, was the key to Moses' extraordinary feats. After his inauguration by God to Moses' seat, that very angel was now making himself known to Joshua to complete the word of the Lord to His people. The angel manifested to show Joshua two very important things. The first one is that Joshua may have lost Moses but nonetheless he was not alone. The Lord and His angel were with the new leader as they had been with his predecessor. [30]

The second thing the angel's appearance conveyed to Joshua (and convinced him of) was the outcome of what he was about to experience in combat. The victories and triumphs that awaited him were not of his own doing. Even if his adversaries did not know it, Joshua was to remain aware that it was the God of Israel and His forces that fought and won his battles. They were

---

[30] Read Genesis 28:12 and 32:1.

responsible for the military conquests he was about to enjoy.[31.] Moses may have left the planet, but the Lord and His hosts had not, and what had seen to Moses' success was poised to back Joshua, Jehovah's newest leader, as well.

When it comes to counting on God's angels' support when He has turned His hand against a particular servant, it is wise to consider this. The Lord's angels have been with Him a long time, long before the world we know came into existence. When they hear Him say to pull back their support or shift it to another, the invisible supernatural strength of God's ministers obey *His* voice and not ours. Their allegiance to any human being is strictly limited to what they are assigned by God to do on His behalf for them. When God shifts to another or commands them to do so, that is what they do regardless of how long it may take the person they once upheld years to discover the change took place. Think of Saul's spiritual power switch. The Lord's assigned spirit was recalled and was replaced with an evil one nearly two decades before the king was physically dethroned. See 1 Samuel 16:14.

Let us look at Israel's first king's reign further as an example. Saul was fired by God and replaced by David about twenty years before anyone outside his closest circle ever got wind of it. When this happened, even Samuel, the Lord's prophet, eventually ceased serving Saul because the Lord commanded him to move onto the king's successor. When God strips a prophet, or any leader for that matter, of His supernatural aid and backing, it

---

[31] See Judges 2:1; 6:11; Genesis 28:12; and John 1:51.

is a crushing experience that paves the way for the servant's darkest and most humiliating hours in God's ministry. That is how Saul ended up at the witch of Endor's house trying to force the Lord's true prophet Samuel to serve him from the grave one more time.

Divine Correction for Dereliction and Idolatry

It is devastating for active prophets to feel that wall go up between themselves and the Lord. By the way, before you let irrational fear and panic take hold of you, realize that none of this happens immediately, nor is it God's common response to unintentional mistakes. He resorts to such tactics only when things really go awry between Himself and His servants. To shake them out of their delusions, the Lord reluctantly withdraws Himself in response to years of deliberate misconduct, disinterest, insincerity, disrespect or disobedience. Once these have replaced the early warm and faithful service the minister previously rendered to Him, God uses stronger measures to make His point.

Serious neglect of one's relationship with the Lord or persisting in the casualness that forgets He is still both God of gods and King of kings can, and will, trigger His silence. When money, prestige, fear of unpopularity or anonymity usurp the Lord's place in anyone's ministry or devotions, God reacts by completely shutting down on the person until his or her godly senses returns. Historically, because He cannot tolerate infidelity or idolatry, even if it is due to family loyalties, scripture shows the Lord over time uses silence as the best way to command an errant servant's attention. When the Lord ceases to perform a prophet's words, to supply him or her with fresh revelation, or to perform spiritually the miraculous words spoken or deeds attempted, then the messenger will make it into His presence for that long awaited meeting. Drying things up sometimes is the only way God can breakthrough to His ministers.

As a rule, the Lord will eventually sever His relations with anyone that affronts His sovereignty and diminishes His royalty and holiness[32]. Regardless of how often the Lord creates and maintains intimate relations with His people, it is still on the basis of His Godhood and majesty as their Lord and Maker. His first and highest standard of treatment from us is that we ever regard Him as holy. God never expects those He grooms to serve Him in any fashion to reduce Him to their standards, or to *commonize* His Deity. He demands to be revered no matter how familiar or relaxed He permits a person to become with Him. This is doubly true when it comes to His ministers, in particular His prophetic ones.

---

[32] See Leviticus 10:1-3.

Chapter Five

Nonstop Communion with the Almighty

Seasoned prophets and devoted worshippers come to rely on their day to day, almost nonstop interactions with the Lord early in their walk with Him. For His future servants, it is essential to their ministry orientation. From the first moment they hear His voice, despite not knowing why, it takes only a short time for such people to become accustomed to it and ultimately to depend wholly upon God's daily presence and constant activity in their lives. Without it, they grow weak, wavering, fearful, and intimidated by everything they once dominated or were being taught by the Savior to dominate. Eventually, young prophetic ministers grow to need the sound of God's voice in their ears the way a babe needs to hear his or her parent. More than their daily sustenance, prophets need to feel the Lord's presence and overtures in their lives. In no time at all, it becomes their daily bread. Being taken into the Lord's confidences or participating in His discussions with His spiritual agents[33] on matters of heavenly concern is not only heady, it quickly becomes addictive,[34, 35] which is how the Lord designed it to be between Himself and His servants.

Ministry addiction[36], something the modern church scorns, is what gives prophets (and other potent leaders) their edge as God's supernatural intelligence force[37]. Growing increasingly reliant upon His voice is what establishes a messenger as one of the Lord's trusted communicators. When God awakens a prophet, He swiftly and aggressively fuses a binding core between them that creates a healthy and deliberate spiritual co-dependency. Should anything happen to splinter what binds them, it will destroy the prophet, perhaps more than the other ministries, because God's silence invariably conveys the prophet's separation from His service, temporarily or permanently. Remember, the most succinct definition of a prophet is that *"he or she is the earthly voice of a deity's thoughts, will, actions, and intents."* Keeping that definition in mind will make this

---

[33] See Zechariah 3:1-10.

[34] Paul uses this term in 1 Corinthians 16:15.

[35] From the Greek *tasso*: to arrange in an orderly manner in order to assign or dispose to a certain position or lot; to addict to an appointment as determined by ordination; to set (as in install or instate). Refers to being devoted, yielded to declare or deliver a declaration; totally surrendered to some practice or habit.

[36] An addiction is most succinctly defined as a habitual, compulsion, a craving, and a dependency.

[37] See Deuteronomy 4:1-9.

discussion even clearer to you. Without a deity to speak for, one must ask, "whose thoughts the prophet is voicing?"

On the basis of that definition, the Lord's refusal to talk with a minister that He has made dependent upon the sound of His voice and the manifestation of His deeds equates to a heartrending rejection of the person's ministry. There can be no other interpretation of God's prolonged silence than that He has decided to cease using a particular messenger to speak on His behalf. What makes this even more tragic in the prophet's life is how the Lord inducted the minister into His service. It is according to Numbers 12:6. The way it describes a prophet's induction is what makes the absence of God's communications sorely missed when it happens. In accustoming the messenger to His interaction, the Lord merges His own makeup with the new messenger's[38] to solidify the reality that He indeed made the prophet His official spokesperson. Here is how it is done. To acquaint newcomers to His service with Himself, the Lord goes to great lengths to settle the fresh voice in His daily dynamics.

The initiation process to God's service most notably involves getting newcomers comfortable with being up close and personal with Him, and making them reliant upon a close personal union with the Almighty to the point that they need it all the time. Hence, the addiction piece. Since moments with God are so fulfilling and enriching to the truly prophetic soul, it does not take long to get used to His intense intimacy and powerful dealings. Should these lofty experiences abruptly stop, life grows

---

[38] See Nehemiah 9:30.

dark and hollow for the prophet as God's inescapable silence creates a vacuum type sensation within. As a result, the prophet above all other servants, can feel doomed while he or she lives because of the seemingly endless chasm the Lord's silence causes between them. For the prophetic soul, there is just no harsher judgment than God inexplicably ceasing to communicate after years of hearty interaction. While it bothers all believers, it breeds an especially inconsolable soul-ache in prophets that intensifies when they are forced to accept that the Lord is determined to rebuff any of their efforts to reach out to Him. Eventually, the hurt deepens as they realize He remains unmoved by their appeals. From then on, the quest of these prophets turns to finding out why God stopped talking and will not resume, even if they keep it a secret. Going from offender to defender, the journey to find out what happened between them and God takes some prophets on a long path to discover what provoked the Lord to cut off their relations. In the end, the message becomes clear. Although God only resorts to such extreme behavior for very good reasons, these prophets have made the mistake of giving Him one of those reasons. The only solution at this point is to acknowledge whatever offense caused the rift, repent and return things to how they were before the conflict. Thank God for His mercy and grace.

Unfortunately, though, many seasoned veterans of the mantle will not initiate or follow through on the requirements for restoring their fellowship with God. For many of them, the cost is too great and the stakes of a long and successful ministry can make it too high. The scenario for these prophets is quite different. They excuse, explain, and justify their strained relations with the Lord. They marginalize His word and righteousness and eventually replace His silence with divination, believing no one can really discern the difference outside of them. Their messages turn from God to man; their testimonies switch from Christ to themselves; and their predictions cease to be scripture based. God's distance makes them downgrade their prophesying to sheer fortune telling. Like Balaam, these spiritually barren messengers eventually hire themselves and their services out to the highest bidder and another false prophet or teacher is born[39]. You can complete the end of the story. For biblical examples of this age old contest between the Lord, His prophets, and His adversaries, recall the lying prophet in 1 Kings 13; of course Balaam[40]; and in the New Testament, Barjesus, the false prophet[41].

When God Seems Harsh, Indifferent, or Brutal

Any extreme adversity from God is unquestionably brought on by extreme worshipper or servant offenses that have morphed into full-blown idolatry. No one knows this better than the prophets themselves distance and silence are His typical responses to it. As a matter of fact, their preparatory training with the Lord includes strong admonitions and disciplinary measures that warn His prophetic learners against taking Him for granted. During their training, God imposes sometimes enigmatically harsh object

---

[39] Study 1 Kings 9:20.
[40] Review Numbers 22-30; Deuteronomy 23:4, 5; Joshua 13:22; 24:9, 10; Nehemiah 13:13.
[41] See Acts 13:6.

lessons on His trainee prophets to etch His relational boundaries in their hearts and minds. Take Balaam's donkey that nearly crushing his foot and the angel with sword drawn ready to take his life as examples. Using numerous humiliating and excruciating drills and simulations, the Lord embeds in all His prophets' souls the weighty cost of betraying Him.[42] Some warnings are subliminally embedded in their consciousness to be used later to trigger specific reminders that warn them against potentially dangerous acts or beliefs that amount to rebellion against Him. Many a prophet can recall God's indisputably rough treatment in some of these classes and how their chastening served to remove any thought of foolhardiness from them in the future.

The Lord's spiritual exchanges with His prophets always deposit a vast richness in their souls because prophetic communion is intended to be more than pleasantly sensuous divine encounters with Him, so to speak. They are never chance revelries to amuse the prophet's senses, but rather preludes to a deliberate conference with God in His closed chambers whereby He implants His seeds of truth, revelation, and prophecy within their unique prophets' spirits for future service to Him. As the training progresses, the Lord draws on these to empower, equip, and enrich the prophet for decades of prophetic ministry assignments. Because of this, it can take a long while for a prophet, or any minister, to connect a single ministerial offense to

---

[42] See Hebrews 10:31; Romans 11:22.

When God Goes Silent

God's withdrawal of His grace or support. For numerous messengers in God's active service today, such consequences have yet to become noticeable or felt because of the richness of their early communion with Him during their formative years as His ministerial trainees. So fruitful were those hours of incubator intimacy that the material harvests they germinated yields to them for decades. So it could take many years to exhaust this harvest before wayward ministers actually realize that they and the Lord developed issues between them and their ministries are on His chopping block.

During those formative years, the Lord forges an almost invincible shield about His future messengers that guards them and their ministries for decades.[43] This is in spite of the early training trials intended to condition them for what lies ahead as His future ministers. For a long time into the ministry, those early divine shields support God's need for a servant by temporarily covering many offenses, spiritual blunders, if you will. He does this to forestall the normal devastations associated with brash and brazen service in His name so they do not exact revenge upon a minister for disobedience before He is ready to recompense it. The outcome of the postponement is a delay of His ordinary judgment on serious offenses committed by presumptuous servants in His service. God's motive in these cases is His bigger picture. He stays

---

[43] Think about Satan's charge against God concerning His servant Job. The devil complained that the Lord had made Job so invincible he could not get to him to carry out his temptation. To accommodate the devil, the Lord lifted Job's hedge of protection that was given to him to guarantee his service to the Most High God.

the hand of judgment to complete the purpose for which He raised up the work in the first place.

When and Why Divine Judgment Is Delayed

For the sake of expediency, the Lord tends to reserve His most crippling discipline for more opportune times should they become necessary.[44] When the time for chastening arrives, the initial grace that supplied the work gets used up by service requirements, imprudent excesses, lack of good judgment, and withheld divine replenishment. However, years of impenitence can completely forfeit His grace supply if it is not addressed at the time the offenses were committed or soon after. Ministers who fail to resolve their issues with the Lord during their ministries' peak years end their service indebted to His righteousness. That means outstanding corrections of unresolved offenses come due often after the minister's cushion of grace wanes[45]. These recompenses surface in the form of chastisement such as sudden inexplicable impoverishment, prolonged illness, thorny domestic or other woes, afflictions or societal conflicts that refuse to be resolved.

Over time, as the minister's initial dispensation expends itself and is not replenished by the Lord, his or her moment of judgment inevitably arrives so that what must be repented of and dealt with on earth is not carried over to the servant's eternal life. It is not uncommon for delayed consequences to begin long after the minister's preparatory stock of grace is depleted because

---

[44] See Exodus 32:34.
[45] Refer to Galatians 6:3-10.

accomplishing the minister's reason for being inducted into God's service and appointed to His ministry takes precedence for a while. Once the reason for keeping the ministry strong and vibrant for the decades it took to fulfill its earthly purpose expires, the acts that were never resolved that courted the Lord's displeasure come to fore[46]. Unfortunately, this typically occurs after the minister's natural and spiritual assets are depleted as well. Taking advantage of the messenger's now drained grace supply; trials aimed at correcting earlier trivialized and unrepented offenses ensue, usually long after many years of seemingly successful service to the Lord have been rendered. At this point, veteran servants' personal and individual resources are too skimpy to cope with God's long overdue chastisement on an earlier youthful offense and so it appears more severe than necessary at first. When this happens, faithful ministers' golden years seem to come under unfair attack as God's well-deserved discipline runs its course.

The Lord has a pervasive inescapable justice system that supersedes all earthly and human governments. Its invisible justices administrate His laws despite what world authorities say or legislate. Refer back to Nebuchadnezzar's experience when he bucked against the Most High's authorities. Review His account in Daniel chapter four, and then compare its reasoning with 1 Timothy 5:24 *"Some men's sins are clearly evident, preceding them to judgment, but those of some men follow later. 25 Likewise, the good works of some are clearly evident, and those that are otherwise cannot be*

---

[46] See Amos 3:14.

hidden". NKJV[47] All of this is to say that God wants His scales of justice on a life to balance before it ends. If it does not, then offenses committed on earth will go with the servant into the afterlife to be judged. There they will not be so graciously dealt with because outside of this world penalties and rewards are the issue and not repentance.[48]" God's divine justice system then seeks to adjudicate offenses that occur early His servant's lives as was the case with King Saul, Israel's first monarch.[49] If He does not permit it then, it is because His heavenly judiciary feel it is useless to remediate the person's sins because his or her loss of reward on account of it is just and should stand forever. Divine Justice's duty, a topic rarely addressed in the church today, is to see that everyone dies with their righteousness account settled.[50] One way or another, this detail happens to resolve impenitence and to reward the faithfulness done in a body before its spirit and soul leave the planet. It does not matter which one it is; the end result is the same. Every person's sins and works will follow his or her death into the afterlife to be handled by the only judge between God and man, the Man Christ Jesus. See 2 Corinthians 5:10; 2 Timothy 4:1; 1 Peter 1:5; and 1 Timothy 5:4.

To the outsiders who supported a chastised minister's ministry over the years, it can look as if the Lord rewarded years of faithful service with evil, cruelly punishing a devoted and

---

[47] "Remember that some people lead sinful lives, and everyone knows they will be judged. But there are others whose sin will not be revealed until later." NLT
[48] See 1 Corinthians 3:10-15.
[49] See Ezekiel 3:20 and 18:24, 26.
[50] See Daniel chapter 5.

successful minister for no apparent reason. What usually happens in these cases is that a minister's spiritual stockpile of mercy runs out as he or she ages, leaving him or her with too little righteousness and spiritual fortitude to deal with God's late in life justice on an earlier disobedience. Not to mention that a refusal to repent leaves Him with no recourse but to settle matters later in a life. As a result, the closing years can be devastating[51]. With all the grace and spiritual resources of the early years gone, God's correction has a greater impact, although it seems unwarranted and unreasonable to the uninformed. Before you criticize this practice of God's, remember this. Only the Almighty is in a person's life twenty-four hours a day, seven days a week, three hundred sixty-five days a year. He alone witnesses what people do out of the public's eye and what they vow in their hearts concerning Him.[52] In light of this insight, it is risky to assume the Lord has wrongly treated someone that you admire just because you do not know how or when they offended Him over the years of their supposed loyal service. At the very least, the Lord says His judgment is to instill His fear in the righteous. It is also reckless on your part to attribute God's righteous judgment to the devil. Even when it comes to divine chastening, the Lord is adamant about His glory never being given to another. He takes full responsibility and credit for all His actions. To ascribe His just recompenses to Satan is to imply that God's righteousness is inconsequential and sin is not to be repented of when it is

---

[51] Read what the Lord Jesus wrote to His angel over the church in Thyatira concerning Jezebel the false prophetess who was apparently over it.
[52] Refer to Ezekiel 8:1-13.

committed. It is also to say that the devil is stronger than his Maker and is completely out of the Almighty's control. None of this is true. If you do not understand the bad things that happen to supposedly good people, pray about it, study God's word, but most of all count the Lord righteous and just because Job says the Almighty cannot do wickedness or commit iniquity. *"Therefore hearken unto me, ye men of understanding: far be it from God, that he should do wickedness; and from the Almighty, that he should commit iniquity."* Job 34:10, KJV.

Do Not Panic Yet

Before you panic and begin to look for this type of treatment from the Lord yourself, bear in mind that His sense of justice always motivates Him to warn people repeatedly before He acts in any way. This is particularly true with His delinquent ministers because He needs more of them on His staff and not less. Frequently, the Lord will at first alert them to His feelings in dreams and visions[53]. When that approach fails, He will then send His prophets mentors, peers, or colleagues to inform people they are treading on thin ice with Him. Sometimes God will announce His displeasure for years before its actual consequences are experienced. Unfortunately, it seems the more He announces His intent to judge, and then forestalls His judgment, the more those He tries to reach take His presumed silence on their sin as approval and choose to ignore Him. Often ministers become so comfortable when the prosperous lifestyles that overlay their

---

[53] Job 33:14-18.

When God Goes Silent

ministerial misconduct they assume divine service exempts them from repentance and makes them impervious to God's judgment on their unrighteousness. At other times, they just conclude the cost or risk of repentance is more damaging to them at the moment than God's reaction to their misconduct in His service. They opt to take a wait-and-see attitude that hopes the scales of the Lord's divine justice concerning them balance out in their favor on their own down the line. Of course our righteous God cannot let that happen.

Chapter Six
The Pain of God's Silent Treatment

For the active prophet who truly wears the resurrected Jesus' prophetic mantle of service, God's going silent ushers in the most painful (and darkest) period in life. Almost compulsively, the first response of many prophets is to hide the inward suffering because only a handful of them feel safe enough to dare confide it to others. Most prophets, ministers, or saints today walking around wrestling with God's sentence of silence on their lives, for understandable reasons, resolve not to reveal it to anyone for fear of the consequences that can compound their problem. If they want to continue being sought after and respected for the word of the Lord, they cannot let on that God is no longer sharing His thoughts with them. That would be damaging to their reputations, crippling to their ministries, and devastating to their economies. The worst part of it all is that for these reasons a prophet can find little sympathy for his or her plight or insight on how to end it. After all, who wants to learn that a prophet one esteems has ceased hearing from the God one serves? That cannot be, since people, as they are rightfully supposed to do so by the Lord, rely on His prophets to hear from Him and to convey what they need Him to hear on their behalf. Whether they believe prophets should legitimately exist or not, those who have remotely heard anything about them know that God and prophets should always be on speaking terms. Understandably in their minds the two, God and His mouthpieces, should be in constant communion, which is why petitioners can expect their names or situations to come up in conversations between them.

The very reason people regard prophets in the first place is to initiate and maintain an association with them that increases their odds of being heard and responded to by God. Presumably, through prophets' interactions with the Lord the answers His children cannot seem to get or comprehend on their own are released, or clarified. Truly convinced believers depend on prophets' intercessory and interventional privileges with God to benefit them at some time or another. People trust prophets' special occupational status with God to keep them informed of His mind and doings in their lives, and their issues ever before Him[54]. That cannot happen if the Lord shuts His ears to a prophet's voice.

---

[54] See Exodus 18:13-27.

As mediatorial representatives of their concerns to the Lord, people look to the prophets in their lives to hear from God and bring back to them the word they need from the Lord to act according to His will. Those who have significant experience with prophets and prophecies know the seasoned prophet's word will encompass more than predictions. Well-oriented members of Christ's body know that they can anticipate wisdom, guidance, counsel, and divine instruction as well as correction to come from a respectable prophet's mouth. If any of you are only receiving predictions from the prophets you entreat, then you are probably not dealing with an official prophet, but most likely a prophesier; a minister with no significant license with the Lord.

With these explanations in mind, you can see how troubling it is for ministers and their audiences or charges to have the Lord to stop talking with a once prolific servant. Under such circumstances, a normally conversant messenger can no longer receive prophetic or even insightful words from Him for others. For a prophet to reveal this to most people is for the prophet to announce that God has effectively disemployed his or her mantle. Because of this, those caught in the grip of this dilemma will rarely admit it. To say that it has been a long time since the Lord said anything to them is to jeopardize seriously their way of life. Beyond that, history has shown many of them that the few ministers who attempted to confide such a thing are scorned, judged, mocked, or shunned. So they learn from early experience or by watching the fallout from others who tried to be "transparent" that it is a dangerous thing to do. Public ministers

wishing to share their issues and seek comfort and advice understand that to do so with the average Christian should not always expect to be consoled for it. That can be naïve. This reality unfortunately leaves the "blacklisted" messenger to wander through life pretending and agonizing day after day over God's incomprehensible silence.

The Effects of God's Silent Treatment

God's silent treatment can create a very lonely world for a prophet, or any minister for that matter, especially His leaders. When it happens, some of them get worn out with wrestling with it in secret for years, never being able to seek help from others. To glimpse what such an existence looks like from the inside, think about Saul, Israel's first king. He failed God because he trivialized three things that the Lord held dear: His beloved kingdom, His holy word, and His sanctified Priesthood.[55]

When Saul violated God's Priesthood and disobeyed His command, the Lord reacted to his misconduct harshly because he stood in authority over His people. As king, his disobedience would (and eventually did) seriously pervert them. Saul's presumption exposed his disrespect for what the Lord decreed as holy to Him. That disrespect, when observed by followers, authorizes them to treat His hallowed priestly institution as common and His ministrations with contempt. In light of this, it follows then that God cannot respect or trust a servant who

---

[55] See 1 Samuel 13:8-14; 14:35; and chapter 15.

cannot or will not perform one hundred percent of what He needs and wants in office and on assignment. In a similar vein, the implications of a ministers, particularly prophet's, recurring misbehavior are too immense for the Lord to overlook because He has told His people to look to His offices for guidance, truth, and instruction in His righteousness. After a verified track record of hearing and responding inaccurately to what the Lord says and other repeated violations, such ministers are recorded by Him as irremediably errant and rebellious. Their constantly insolent service leaves God with no alternative but to cease expecting them to represent Him responsibly. In such cases, He has no other option but to react that way because God just cannot risk the cost of continually dispatching unstable ministers in His service to perform what He sends them to do for Him incorrectly. Consequently, the best thing He can do for His mission and His people is to transfer the wayward servant's mantle resources to one who is more reliable and steadfast, which is what He did with David and Saul as recorded in 1 Samuel 13:13, 14.

To avert the rippling effect of ministerial misconduct and its detriments in His body, God, like any prudent leader, demotes the incapable and replaces them with the most competent. When this problem occurs organizationally on a large scale, the Lord simply shuts down the entire ministry altogether until His chosen replacement is born, groomed and ready to rectify the situation for Him. You may see these people continuing to go on as if nothing happened and begin to suspect your detection of their errancy was inaccurate, but just wait. If you are correct and your conclusion was based on God's Spirit and word of truth, what they are hiding will eventually surface. Actually, in today's church, this is a chronic problem for the Lord as we routinely see global ministries once faithful to the Lord turned to darkness. We wonder why the Lord will not do anything about it. There are many answers to this question, but the most glaring one is that His people keep supporting their sin and incompetence despite their abandoned fidelity and devotion to God in His service. It is amazing how deluded Christians continue to sow seed and sacrifice to minister's whose service blatantly disdains the Lord's truth. And they wonder why they cannot hear God or what made Him stop talking to them. The Lord, on the other hand, is bound to His righteousness and distances Himself from His ungodly servants rather quickly. Unfortunately though, when God departs from a faithless minister, it often takes His people awhile to get the message. Many of them do not get it until they witness the fullness of His judgment upon the minister. Even though what caused Him to do so may have happened a long time ago, that the Lord has distanced Himself does not escape the discerning eye of serious worshippers. These people respond just as quickly when they realized it and immediately stop supporting the errant. We see this with Samuel and Eli discussed later in the book.

The Prophetic Effect of God's Silent Treatment

It is natural for any saint who has ever enjoyed a rich interactive relationship with the Lord to feel hurt if He retreats and refuses to communicate, even if briefly. The most stalwart public minister pines away inside when the Lord first severs relations with him or her. I am sure many believers can (and should be able to) relate to the discomfort of God's going silent on them at least once. I know I can. So it almost goes without saying that a long-term silence from one's God is painful, period! However, at times it is necessary for a variety of reasons for the Lord to restrain communications with His child, at least in the early days of their union.[56] Scripture says the Lord chastens those He loves and scourges every child He receives.[57] That chastening takes many forms. Therefore, it is a foregone conclusion that all of us at one time or another will meet the disciplinary side of God's character, especially in the beginning; I certainly did once. The Lord's holiness teaches all of His children over the years that He is not a God of folly (foolishness); He is a holy God to be worshipped and revered. Correction, chastening, and proving are inherent to our adaptation to God and His kingdom. It is the object and effect of the techniques He uses to make His point that are at issue here. God's normal rule of thumb is this: the more impactful the servant, the more indelible the correction.

The consequences of any corrective experience with God, for the Christian worshipper, though discomforting, is largely confined to devotional relations with Him. Any internal struggle between the Father and His child, as agonizing as it may be, is limited in its effect because private behaviors are less of a threat to His global objectives. He views them similar to how a government

[56] 2 Chronicles 32:31 and Exodus 20:20.
[57] Hebrews 12:5-8.

treats a citizen's misdemeanors and infractions as opposed to those of one of its officials. The professional minister's misconduct in contrast poses a different kind of problem for the Lord. Prophets' public duty to God's body for instance, sets their interactions with Him on an entirely different plane. This is because their very occupation relies on ceaseless communications with and from God. Their times with the Lord are more than devotional experiences to get them through their Christian walk in life. They comprise the business meetings that validate their continuance as His mouthpiece and sustained effectiveness in His service as guardians of His truth and defenders of His righteousness. In contrast, any empathy the typical believer may feel about God's silence cannot equate to the prophet's quiet torment in comparison. This is to say that being unheeded by God in one's prayer closet is not quite as incapacitating as going unheard and unheeded by Him in public ministry, although in all cases it is heart rending.

When God silences His voice to His prophet, it means at the same time that He has chosen to silence His prophet's voice on His behalf as well. However, I want to reiterate that if this happens and continues, it is because the messenger provoked it by ignoring God's voice for some time in the past, or by consistently refusing to do what He says. For examples of prophetic actions that cause the Lord to go silent, see Micah 3:5-7 and Revelation 2:20-23. Both references show that an irreparable breakdown between the Lord and His prophet will close down their communications. When it occurs, the mantle's inherent instincts tell the prophet that God's ongoing silence signals a serious conflict between them that marks a foreboding and perhaps disastrous turn in their relationship. Many of those meeting His wall of silence will notice the difference right away, even if they are unable to say why at first. Others will either shrug it off or be unaware of it entirely.

Specific Clues to God's Silencing a Prophetic Minister

For all of the above reasons, God's ceasing to speak to a prophet immobilizes his or her ministry until the messenger repents or defects. As long as it is in effect, His silent treatment condemns the prophet's words to fail and downgrades predictions to mere divination because His speeches are the sole reason prophets' mantles exist. Also, with the office's purposes and functions being so broad and its responsibilities so weighty, being defined by much more than prophesying. The messenger's public ministrations are likewise adversely affected. To illustrate, you will notice in divinely silenced prophets, and other ministers too, especially teachers, the reduced ability to give the mind of the Lord spontaneously. Repeatedly, in the prophets predictions miss their mark or are applied to the wrong situations. Opinions more and more replace true revelation as hunches and impressions are given to appear prophetic. Often these are accompanied by irrational theatrics or physical antics aimed at convincing witnesses that God is still moving with them. Some of you know what I am talking about. One of the most ludicrous one's I have has seen is the people who constantly jerk and convulse in your presence to alert you that the Holy Spirit is moving upon them. Other antics include constant trembling, jitters, or inane mumbling. In addition to these, various manipulations are engaged in to keep up the façade such as tricks, gimmicks, and trendy devices used to imitate divine communications. Most of all is the doctrine change. Fresh manna gives way to stale bread. Old teachings and expired wisdom are circulated. All in all, the greatest sign is an exit from the true and a return to the old time religion or old eras, revivals, or environments of God's dealings with His people. The most notable one is an exit from grace and a new baptism in the works of the Old Testament law. And then there is a giant leap into the mystical, where the mythical religions of false gods are peddled as enlightened Christianity or a rediscovery of what traditionalism supposedly suppressed as occult. You can tell these events because they are fleshly, familiar, and contradictory to the revealed word of God and established Christian truth. In observation and experience they are drab, weighty, and inconsistent with the character and nature of God's life, light and established revelation. Any combination of these is likely to be at work within or worked by the minister sentenced to God's silent treatment. Some are the cause and the others the result. Either way, the conclusion is the same, God is ignoring His servant and its hurts, but one must go on.

As the situation drags on, prophetic messengers dispense less and less wisdom on modern issues and fewer answers to the questions posed by those seeking the Lord's word on a matter.

Bible references are sporadic and many of those used are just plain errant as wrangled scripture replaces spiritual intelligence. For these reasons, sermons and teachings become cyclical, trendy, and brief while praise and worship services are exaggerated to fill the void. All of this is because the Holy Spirit's customary deluge of God's wisdom and insights are stopped. Criticalness, scorn and mockery replace incisiveness as a bitter cutting edge overlays the affections of a once compassionate ministry. The fruit of the Spirit is absent because jadedness turned previously thoughtful counsel into mysticism. All in all, the mantle's mutation accelerates as its features and faculties progressively decline. The more the minister corrupts the Lord, the word, and works, the faster he or she deteriorates spiritually and eventually in every other way.

Long Term Effects of God's Extended Silence

God's silence is how He dismantles His messengers. The above profile of prophetic deterioration was given to provide you with some signs of the effects of God's silence that you will definitely want to avoid. It is also to help you recognize when others are overcome by God's silence and the resultant muting of their voices as well. The hope is that you will do all you can to protect your calling and be vigilant in securing everything the Lord entrusts to you. Just remember that very few ministers in conflict with the Lord today awoke one morning and said, "I think I'll betray or pervert the Lord today." It happens subtly in the beginning, gradually intensifying until the situation gets out of hand. No one is immune to it. Because the Lord's call to ministry

When God Goes Silent

is imperceptible people tend to think that remaining in His service is easy. Often they find out too late that as with anything else, it takes effort and conscientiousness to remain faithful to God in His service. Forgetting that the prophet's mantle was designed by God to serve as His sentinel, guardian and watchman, intercessor and intervener, governor and legislator at once, uninformed prophets can unwittingly risk His displeasure without meaning to do so. They can do this because they are unaware of what collectively makes up the core of the prophet's office. Keep in mind that there is a reason why the Lord Jesus goes through such effort to exhort us to endure to the end. Casualness and complacency are the two minefields of quality ministry and succumbing to either may keep you before the public, but will remove you from God's staff. After all, one can hardly represent God the way He wants after having fallen out of grace with Him. Treat your service to the invisible God as attentively as you would an earthly ruler and you will be honored and trusted by Him. A lack of awareness, makes many ministers unable to understand why the office and its officers' judgments must be heavy handed. Considering the gravity of the prophet's ministry, it should be easy to see by now why God's retreat from a prophet spells trouble.

The prophetic as an institution forms and superintends the major communications bond between God and His people. It does not matter if it is handled by an official prophet or some other ministry authority; voicing God and keeping people attuned to His voice so they abide in Him preserves them and in turn fosters their intimacy with their Heavenly Father and Jesus Christ. All of this makes rightly representing the Lord consistently the most vital of all God's servants' duty. A tear in the prophet's and God's relationship creates an estrangement that can inspire many of His messengers to seek other sources for their prophetic material. To stay in business, so to speak, abandoned prophets left to their own devices tend to resort to the voices of other spirits for heavenly information to convey to their audiences. They feel forced to do so in order to keep their following. Regrettably, their doing so exposes God's people to the infiltration of other gods and weakens His hold on them. Now, before you think God unjust for abandoning a prophet, remember His silence is always in direct response to the messenger's long term abandonment of Him and His way first. As a rule, the Lord lets years of warnings, chastening, and softer discipline precede His ultimate act of severing ties with an unruly prophet, minister or saint. When these fail, He is obliged by His own righteousness to use stronger measures.

Why Avoid God's Silent Treatment

Deuteronomy 8:3 says, *"Man doth not live by bread only, but by every word that proceedeth out of the mouth of the LORD doth man live"* (KJV). Jesus revives this wisdom in His contest with Satan on the mountain after His forty days of fasting. See Matthew 4:4 and Luke 4:4. Accepting that Jesus appeared on earth as the Great

Prophet[58] that Moses foretold would come makes this principle of God's germane to our point. Our Savior defeated His enemy and protected His calling by using the sword of the Lord, God's word, against him. The nexus of this revelation is not just that Jesus used the scriptures to defeat Satan. It is that the inherent power they possessed succeeded in trumping the devil because it was wielded in righteousness. God's scriptures are truth and their conquering power is the Creator's truth. They worked for Jesus because He entered earth as the Almighty's truth and Satan is the father of lies. "Know thy enemy" to Christ was fortified by first knowing Himself. He, as John's gospel declares, is truth; and Satan, the same gospel writer discloses, is a liar. John actually calls him the father of lies. The only weapon Jesus needed to defeat His archrival then was the extreme antithesis of Himself. He is Satan's antithesis, as the Spirit of truth. It is no different for the Most High's messengers today. To conquer God's enemies, they too must wield the sword of the Spirit, the Spirit of truth that is in righteousness.

To avoid God's silent treatment, prophets have to be savvy when it comes to silencing their enemy, and they must do so with the word of truth. The tactic, you should know, only works through wisdom and revelation, not just by randomly quoting one's favorite Bible passages. There must be a strategic link between the word of the Lord invoked and the particular circumstance and context to which it is applied in action. The power of God's scriptures lays not just in their text, but in their

---

[58] Deuteronomy 18:15; Acts 3:22; 7:37.

right application and accurate truth, something no prophet in God's service can last too long mistaking. To decree, for instance, a harvest is coming on a situation that calls for warfare is futile. In like manner to cast out the devil of a broken heart may make for good show, but it is vain and errant, a complete show of callousness. Actual circumstances must correspond to the scripture passages invoked; otherwise, the inherent power of God's word for a given incident is null and void. This is because prophetic declarations must coincide with their precise biblical remedies. Remember, in the realm of the spirit, it is all about truth, Creator truth. That means prophetic efficacy and competency depend on comprehensive scripture knowledge. Today, far too many prophets do not know the scriptures, which is conflicting because they also claim to speak the word of God at the same time.

Of the many lessons that the wilderness test Jesus passed teaches prophets today, a most important one is that they, like Him, must be adept at iterating God's word. It is the secret to prophetic potency. This is the critical connection between prophet excellence and scripture fluency that must remain inflexible. The prophet needs words from God that actually voice His will and thoughts. To get them, prophets need to know God's thoughts and reproduce His sound when they speak for Him. That begins with knowing the scriptures proficiently. It is how the Lord's messengers get His ear and the ears of His holy angels and other heavenly forces, as well as His people. Without the two, the minister's ability to discharge the office with skill and effectiveness is greatly reduced. Once the Lord refuses to lend His ear to a prophet, He will also close His people's ears to the prophet's mouth. At least He closes the ears of those who faithfully obey Him. The reason is because the Lord does everything by His word and without His word, nothing happens anywhere to anyone in any way. His word is why He installed the ministry of the prophet and prophetic ministers to His service in the first place. They live to communicate His thoughts, mind, will, and deeds, and to wield the power He deposited in His word on earth. Doing so is intrinsic to prophets' spirits, mantles, and ministries. All three thrive on "what thus says, does, wills, and decrees" the Lord. It does not matter if they communicate – prophesy – by interpreting visions and dreams, psalmody, intercession or revelation teaching; it all starts and ends with the word of the Lord. Whether they function in their consultative capacity as councilors, or use other spiritual tools to carry out other official actions, the prophet's spirit once fused with the Almighty subsists on a steady stream of divine communications to fulfill the calling. When that stops, the prophet becomes impotent as God's agent.

Regardless of the method and medium God uses to shut a prophet out of His revelatory streams, the end result is the same. Prophets have nothing to say or do until the Lord Most High speaks to them, and when He does not do so for long periods of time it brings the ministry to a screeching halt. When the Lord stops unveiling His word, works, and will to prophets, they are left to divine (to repeat spiritual words) by the power of another spirit or god. For the one who started out with the true and living God, that is worse than having a natural parent, mentor, and supporter reject you at the same time.

Two Typical Responses to God Going Silent

Being invisible, and to most people inaudible, the Lord's voice is the only consistently tangible connection prophets maintain with Him as their employer, so to speak. In all of my teachings on prophecy and the prophet, the one thing the Lord has me hammer home the most is that prophets are in this world to amplify our imperceptible God's acts, declarations, decrees, and so forth. To have the Lord cut off communications leaves a minister with two disturbing repercussive decisions. The first one is that he or she can come off the scene, seek God's face and press Him to reveal His reason for the cold shoulder. Once He does so, and He has promised in His word that He would, the next step is for the minister to repent and submit to His discipline to learn the right way. Once they have worked out their differences, God and His servant can resume their relationship and the minister return can to active duty. That is, the Lord reopens their communications channel.

The second alternative is more deadly. It involves the messenger simply shrugging off God's separation and going on executing a public ministry of prophesying without a deity, or without the true God to back the prophecies uttered. Essentially, this involves the prophet transferring his ministry resources to the power of another god. This scenario courts the services of fallen angels to assume the role of Almighty God in the prophet's ministry. Hence, the word *divination*. In God's mind under the Christ dispensation, supernaturally speaking, delivering any divine utterance that the Almighty and His Son Jesus Christ did not speak equates to divination — prophesying by the power, and according to the will, of another god, a divine being. While the first option is merely humiliating for a time, the second one is most tragic. The eventual calamity caused by the second alternative comes from the prophet choosing to follow a course of action that relies solely on willful self-delusion. At the outset, this may or may not have apparent results that can be directly traced back to the prophet's decision. As you read on, you may see it all differently. To explain, some prophets under these conditions must delude themselves into thinking that the true and living God is still speaking to and through them, even though in their hearts they know it is not true. To maintain their following they must deceive the Lord's people into ignoring the nuance (or radical) changes that progressively take place in their ministries. Scripture is full of those who have fallen prey to this fatal seduction. Study for example, Jeroboam[59] in 1 Kings 11-13; Ezekiel chapters 13 and 14; along with Jeremiah 23. Also, read about Ahab and Jezebel, with whom most of us are well acquainted, and Manasseh, Judah's fourteenth king. All of these examples show that there are only two ways to live life on earth: the Almighty God's way or the way of His adversary Satan. Because of God's

---

[59] Jeroboam turned from God to serve demons, as the 1 Chronicles version of the 1 Kings account shows, because he feared people leaving him to serve the true.

unending battle with other gods, really fallen angels pretending to be gods, prophets at every critical stage of their ministries must reinforce their decision to remain faithful to the true and living God. If they seriously waver once, the insidious infiltrations of their enemy can creep in to spoil their mantles. One of the ways I have seen true messengers fall victim to this is when they spend hours and hours investigating other religions, communing with opposing ministers, or indulging cultural differences that plainly conflict with the Lord, and not give anywhere near the same amount of time to actually studying God's word. Over time, excessive encounters with adversarial viewpoints saturate their spirits and psyches with questions and curiosities that grow into full blown contests of their faith. Eventually human and demonic wisdom wages war against God and His wisdom and constant clashes between God's truth and the devil's lies multiply. It is true, a little leaven really does leaven the whole lump. That means a mere speck of falsehood can poison an entire revelation.

Chapter Seven
Example 1: Eli & His Sons

The Old Testament that many New Testament Christians scorn or ignore is full of examples of the Lord having to wrestle other gods and their religions for the souls of His people. Take for instance Eli, the High Priest, in the book of 1 Samuel. His indulgence led God to blend the priesthood with the prophetic through Samuel, his young mentee. Eli's story may not be fully narrated in scripture, but the events that shaped his career and immortalized his deviant service are pretty easy to deduce. In 1 Samuel, Eli has grown fat in his old age. Spiritual obesity as well as natural obesity have taken hold of him. Fat, in spiritual contexts, means excessively carnal. His inner and outward obesity led to the self-indulgence that caused him to lower the bar (standards) of God's service. Although He leaves Eli at his station, God has resolved to nurture the High Priest's replacement because of his poor stewardship over the priesthood. Hannah's prayer and Samuel's subsequent conception reveal how long the Lord suffered with Eli before He could replace him.

Eli's Downward Spiral

Something tragic must have happened to Eli during his early ministry for him to lose his zeal and just go through the motions of apathetically officiating his priesthood. Something insurmountable inspired his rank disregard for God's reverence and priestly law. His response to the news that the ark was taken indicates that he still cared for the Lord, but something more wounding caused him to just give up in his soul and cease to hold the fort any longer. Perhaps after inaugurating his sons to succeed him, he felt powerless to curtail their abuses, although they had to have gotten the boldness to behave the way they did from their home life with their father somewhere along the line. Anyway, Eli's faith and hope in the spirit and value of his call somehow died and along with it, his zeal, excellence, and diligence. The man evidently became cynical, perhaps by too much criticism or maybe by what he perceived to be the futility of his ministry in relation to his beloved nation's sacrilege. Whichever it was, the message comes through loud and clear in his sons' maltreatment of the Lord's people and perversion of the priesthood. God no longer mattered, His offerings and collections would now be the private stash of the priests themselves. It was a dismal time for the Lord and His people, but He had a plan that He simply had to wait it out to implement.

God's Ongoing Struggle for the Faith of His People

Repeatedly the book of Judges shows how God routinely had to raise up potent military figures called judges to rescue His people from invading nations and their gods. Time and again, He had to do so to restore their faith in Him and return them to His pure worship. Every time He did, for a few decades it seemed to work. During that time, His people responded penitently to His deliverances and rewarded His favor and good graces with revival. For a season, they rejoiced over their deliverance from their captors and briefly relished Yahweh's again flexing His muscles on their behalf. To show their appreciation, they vowed to turn and remain with Him, and fully resume their true faith and covenantal worship, but it was always short-lived. They could not resist the temptation to indulge their inner lusts for long and promptly returned to the wickedness of other gods. Although the Lord knew it before it happened, He still periodically sent them deliverers to give them another chance to do things His way. They always failed Him after awhile and drove themselves back into captivity. The cycle was incessant, until God finally removed them from His land.

His primary motive for continuing to rescue His people was to avert their annihilation, which would have surely happened at the hand of their captors had their covenant God not intervened for their salvation. While their shallow faith lasted though, He enjoyed their efforts and rewarded them with temporary respites from their bondage. Momentarily, His blessings and provisions rained on them until they reverted and forced the cycle to repeat itself. With their captors defeated, God's people once more witnessed their God's superiority over the gods they abandoned Him for, and remembered His dominion over the works of His hands. Even if it was, for them only a fleeting experience. The accompanying exultation over being liberated from their enemies temporarily rejuvenates the nation until resentment of God's standards set in again. The wheel that repeats the pattern winds up and their recurring tussle with their Covenant God's holiness begins anew. Over and over Yahweh's mercy and incomprehensible love for His nation overcomes Him and He dispatches one militant judicial figure after another to deliver His repeatedly oppressed nation. Their chronic disobedience however assures the story always ended the same way. Once free, they predictably grow weary of the Lord's righteousness and hallowed theocracy. The pleasures of sin for a season creep in to cloud their judgment and erase the memory of what it was like before the last judge set them free. Getting fed up with Him causes the people to race back into the beguiling arms of their captors and their gods. God's people's brief delight over their short-lived freedom from Him along with their fascination with the ways of the world around them wanes. In its place, a pathetic recall of how bad those dark years really were resurfaces and their confidence in their independence from God melts away. For yet another time, they find themselves the subjects of a spiteful nation who hostilely yanks them from the control, safety and prosperity of their covenant God. In no time, they find themselves once more caught in the grip of bondage. Their new world order quickly reverts to the old world order that reigned before the Lord set them free the last time. They groan under their captor's cruelty and abominable treatment and beg Him to do it again. Typically, a couple of decades pass before the Lord intervenes anew, usually when He just cannot bear His people's groaning and abuse any longer. At this point, He raises up a new judge to rescue them. After He does so, the people renew their covenant, make fresh vows, and temporarily support the ministers of the temple. For a short time, they care about Him and His priests' sustenance and survival. That is until the appeal of the other gods' phony liberty entices them to revive their catastrophic cycle. This historical pattern is pretty much what priests like Eli had come to expect. It may be what embittered his service to the Lord. Years of witnessing this repetitive cycle surely had to take its toll on him, no matter how genuine his original service vows may have been.

No doubt, after awhile Eli ceased to be deluded about the nation that continually forced its Lord to wrought new deliverances for them to prove He was indeed the most powerful God and worthy of the worship they so casually sold to anything spiritual. Although their momentary gratitude moves them to commit to their God periodically in return for His latest deliverance, the cost of living up to their promises invariably becomes, in their minds, just too great. The appeal of the business opportunities, political alliances, orgies, intoxication, and the drugs required, and permitted, by other deities to worship them was just too deeply ingrained in their souls. Years of Egypt's rituals, and the perverse religions of the other nations, bred insatiable appetites for vileness in them that could not be denied for very long. Their souls were addicted to it, and for the most part the war-weary, faithless country was just too powerless to fight it. Inevitably, the call of their godless passions won out and they resold themselves to sin. The reason is surrendering to their covenant God in return for His deliverance meant they could no longer indulge their godless bloodthirsty appetites for lust, fornication, animal sacrifices, and demonic powers. His deliverances always came with a price. They always forced them to abandon their godless alliances and trust the Almighty to put them over the top without them. That called for a faith in Him that the nation never could quite muster. So the momentary relief they got from Him as pleasant and desirable as it was for awhile never held for long. In no time at all, being conditioned by decades of depravity, their craving for spiritual and moral uncleanness resurfaced and they turned their back on the Lord and His faithful servants over and over again. The routine is quite pitiful. Every time the dire and deadly consequences of their rejection of God took hold, His were crushed under hostile oppression. Only then would they cry out to the Lord to rescue them and He always did. After their rescue, they made more insincere promises to change and put forth serious efforts to do so. However, in the end, it just was not in them. The wild call of the decadent gods that constantly haunted them always won out, they raced back to them to gratify their sinful lusts. This is the world that Eli and his staff of priests faced and mediated for continually.

Eli's Ministerial Climate

Eli knows the routine all too well. First comes the deliverance, and revival almost immediately follows. In no time though, insatiable cravings for the old lead to a spiritual relapse that enslaves his beloved nation to the paganism of the Lord's enemies for another one to three decades. Undoubtedly, their habitual backsliding weighs heavy on the man. After awhile Eli knows what to expect from their feigned repentance and begins to wonder what it (his ministry) is all about after all. Somewhere along the way, though, Eli stopped asking the right questions and began living by the wrong answers. Instead of admonishing the people and maintaining his faith, he permits his sons to take over and run the priesthood into the ground. They perverted it according to their arrogant lusts. Instead of upholding the dignity of the Lord's ministry as was his duty according to Moses' law, Eli responded to his countrymen's depravity by breaking his vow to keep God's charge pure. It became only perfunctory to him. In time, Eli probably began to empathize or sympathize with Israel's unfaithfulness, wondering where it was all going to end, if at all. Besides, there were more of them than Eli, and God appeared to be uninvolved, maybe He was oblivious to the matter altogether.

Eli also seems to have made another fatal ministerial mistake. He apparently shared his ministry bitterness with his family, especially his sons as youngsters. Perhaps he sat around the dinner table with them bemoaning one unhappy or disappointing incident after another over the years. His sons, hearing him moan and complain about the futility of his call and the frustrations of serving an obviously thankless Jehovah, were brought into their father's bitterness and began to resent the Lord and His ministry as well. Perhaps they thought, "How good can it be to serve the Lord when it made their dad so miserable?" And besides, they no doubt wondered, "What kind of God would impose such hardship upon their clearly faithful father's service?" For sure, none of it made too much sense to the youngsters and as kids do, they took their dad's word for it and became brainwashed against the Lord at his word. Apparently, at some point in their formative years they made heart vows to not let what happened to their father happen to them.

The Danger of Self-Pity in Ministry

As is common with many severely tried ministers, even today, Eli most likely blamed God and His priesthood (outwardly or not) for many of the family struggles. During the times when the nation suffered for rejecting its God and famine set in, the priests were invariably were among the hardest hit. The people's lack certainly shrunk their giving in response. That meant a definite decrease in the family's economy, which in turn left little for the extras, and probably the necessities, they needed to thrive. Their family's lack perhaps drove Eli to let the children know how he would have provided for them and given them nice things if it were not for the poverty associated with the priesthood that could be blamed on God's judgment. Eli's complaint evidently bred animosity and resentment in the youngsters toward their God. Decades of watching people's ingratitude toward their father's service and their family's unappreciated sacrifices could not help but further poison the boys and convince them that the ministry was the reason they grew up poor and suffering. When they got grown and held the office, they would not repeat their father's mistake, none of what destroyed him would happen to them. They would never allow the Lord's people to treat them as doormats and they would get their due. Heart vows made as youngsters played out in real life. Bitterness and rage were evidently what their father passed onto his sons about the priesthood above all else.

Inflamed by the years of their father's agonizing over his call, and listening to his feelings of frustration and futility, the boys grew up overwhelmed by it all. Whether or not he exaggerated the matter or presented his performance as greater than it was, Eli's sons developed a severe problem with their father's God. In their minds, his religion and faith had failed him and them. In response, Eli's sons fumed inside and meditated on how not to suffer in God's service as their father had, vowing in their hearts to take matters into their own hands. Eli probably never understood what made his children so irreverent. As time passed, he possibly forgot what he spewed out of his mouth about his ministry and their household lack or struggles while they were growing up. He may never have understood that children hear and respond to parental suffering traumatically. It is questionable as to whether or not Eli ever took responsibility for his sons' distaste for their father's call. For sure, they knew his destiny was theirs because they were Aaronic Levites. Being filled with their witness of their father's misery, Eli's sons apparently hatched a plan. When they entered the ministry, they would make sure their lives as God's ministers did not mirror their dad's. They were smarter, more callous, and had over the years cultivated higher preservation instincts. They were forewarned and therefore forearmed and would not lack or be deprived or abused as priests, not even by the Lord of the priesthood. Maybe Eli never considered the cost of publicizing his private issues with God to his family and how burdensome it was to the young men. He may have dismissed the possibility that their love for their father would cause his mistreatment by God's people to enrage them, and motivate them to blaspheme and defile God's priesthood. Expressly stated or not, it is apparent that their vile handling of their priestly service along with their plundering of the Lord's offerings is definite proof that Eli's resentment contaminated them. Perhaps his later realization of this truth made him too guilty to correct their abominable behavior toward their country's God. If indeed Eli ever recognized that he fed his sons the animosity they held toward the ministry and the Lord, he may have felt that it was too late to reverse it, the damage was done and he could do little to change the situation. Knowing God's character and His sense of justice as we do, it is safe to assume that He reached out to Eli about His sons on numerous occasions. In fact, the unnamed prophet that rebuked him for their atrocities said as much. What is indisputable though, is that as soon as Eli's sons were old enough to make the decision for themselves, they abandoned Israel's true faith to serve the gods of the nations that constantly seduced and enslaved them. As a result, they did not value the spiritual platform and sanctity of their nation's pure religious worship and ritual. Instead, they concluded their priestly ministrations could be just as easily transferred to any deity they chose, and the record shows they did not choose the God of their father or forefathers. That they went from bad to worse proves their father, the High Priest had lost all control over them[60].

Apparently, Eli was still serving when Hannah, the great prophet Samuel's mother went to pray to conceive her son. It may be that his sons were already in God's service by then. Phinehas and Hophni, Eli's two sons, were crude and brutal boys. They were sacrilegious, perverse, fraudulent and abominable. Their contempt for God's priestly office, its service and sacrifices was abhorrent. So much so that they publicly humiliated His women by fornicating with them at the altar when they came to sacrifice and worship. These men wanted to let the Lord and all Israel know that they hated God and His priesthood and were going to vindicate the misery their father had endured from it. With the most repugnant acts they could think of, they defiled the nation and their priestly service and treated God's worshippers abominably. By the time things got this bad, Eli has ceased hearing from God. Obviously, it did not matter because God for

---

[60] See 1 Samuel 3:13.

sure had stopped talking to him. That is why He sent the unidentified prophet to prophesy His perpetual judgment on Eli's house[61]. Nothing would ever pacify God's ire toward Eli and his sons and as soon as He could, He planned to obliterate his seed from the earth forever.

Replacing Eli Resumes God's Communication

The first book of Samuel says in chapter 3 that the Lord had once more grown silent. Endless debates and discussions can go on about what corrupted Eli, a presumably ardent worshipper and servant of God to change him from a faithful high priest to a priest of Israel's dreaded high places. The fact remains that he and God suffered a horrific split that cost the nation and his family tree all. In his golden years, Eli had lost his hold on everything except his tutelage of Samuel, the young child he mentored from toddler to adulthood. Miraculously, the youth somehow escaped Eli's worst and absorbed the best of his service. Given the high priest's age and deteriorated physical condition, it was only a matter of time before the reason Samuel was left in his care manifested.

Over the years it took for Eli to get Samuel ready to perform his priestly functions, the clock ticked on his poor parenting, disgusting ministry, and his spiritual neglect of the Lord's temple and people. The final countdown had begun and God was about to recompense Eli's revolting servitude on

---

[61] Study 1 Samuel chapters 2 and 3.

himself, his sons, and their posterity. Over time his psycho-emotional condition seared his sons' consciousnesses and robbed them of any desire to perform his high priestly duties the way God ordained in his stead. As a result, the Lord was about to rid himself of the chronic stench of their sordid behavior and hateful dealings with Him and His worshippers at last. After sending that prophet to voice His ire and impending judgment, God repeats Eli's doomsday prophecy to Samuel, whom He sends to reiterate it to his mentor. But this time God had a new twist in mind. Samuel, Eli's adopted son, so to speak, was to be next in line for the priesthood, despite his father's Ephraimite nativity[62]. The high priest's defilement of the office was far reaching and so infected all the priests that it disqualified every one of Eli's possible successors. An endless depression and lethargy bred the sloth that spoiled all other Levitical candidates making them unfit to inherit his office. So by the time Samuel comes of age, not one of His priestly clan had God's best interests at heart enough to be trusted with the post upon Eli's death or retirement. His unchecked indulgences gave God His more than sufficient reason for sentencing the four of them to die for their crimes.

Enraged for decades by Eli's permissiveness and His people's subsequent misconduct, the Lord suffered in silence until Samuel was ready for Him to act. The time finally came; Eli's protégé would replace him as unofficial high priest, even though

---

[62]Perhaps his mother Hannah was a Levite. The text does not say. However, the Old Testament shows that the Lord tracks priestly lineage from the father, so Samuel's dad was an Ephraimite. See 1 Samuel 1:1.

he was not a native Levite[63]. By an act of sovereign decree, God etched the Ephraimite Samuel into Israel's priestly order. Effectively neutralizing the Levitical priesthood, He superimposed His contemporaneous will on Moses' unbreakable law. Arrant abuse of His beloved institution by Eli and his sons caused the Lord to shift high priestly service to another tribe temporarily. Eli's dereliction and his sons defection left no one to correct the situation for Him. So, the Lord sovereignly acted to purge His beloved institution Himself by going outside Levi's line for a high priest to minister at His altar. Samuel, it appears, never officially took on the title.[64]

In preparation for the switch, providence installed Samuel in God's temple as a toddler. He was raised in Shiloh from childhood to fulfill two purposes. The primary one was to replace Eli as Israel's unofficial high priest, which effectively blended the offices of priest, prophet, and commander in chief into one. Samuel's secondary purpose was to inaugurate the nation's first professional prophetic institution.[65] Until all of this was ready to transpire, the Lord remained virtually silent on everything that happened in Israel, at least on the national front, as is revealed by 1 Samuel 3:1.

---

[63] It was a matter of record that Samuel was not legitimately born into the Levitical Priesthood according to the Law of Moses (unless Hannah came from a Levitical tribe). Even if Hannah was a Levite, the Law appointed the sons of the father and not the mother. According to scripture, Aaron and his sons inherited the Priesthood, and not their mothers.

[64] That Samuel performed this function is seen in 1 Samuel 13:7-14.

[65] 1 Samuel 1:1-9, KJV.

When God Goes Silent

As you can see from the above account, God's refusal to speak is never without cause, and if He were viewed as a real Person with feelings, likes, dislikes and such, it would be easy to see how wounded He must have been. God's wisdom made Him recognize the uselessness of continuing to speak to a stubborn nation whose calloused ears were deaf to Him. For years, He suffered their uncircumcised hearts' rejection of anything He would say. However, there were prophets in the land at the time because God sent that unnamed one to speak to Eli before Samuel's debut to notify him of his sons' imminent demise. Still, it is obvious that these voices were disrespected and muted by the nation's rejection of its founding God. Strangely, Eli's recorded response to the prophet's word appears to imply that he expected what was prophesied. Maybe in some way he longed for it in order to end the madness. Despite his apathy, as high priest he would have certainly been filled with grief over his sons' actions. Still, decades of leniency cost him their respect and them their lives. So when Eli heard the word of the Lord, he reacted with the ultimate resignation. To paraphrase his attitude, for him it was, "God is right; let His will be done". Perhaps he was a little contrite because he knew he deserved what was prophesied. Overall, though, he seemed to exhibit a type of helplessness that left it all up to God to repair the mess he had made. The negligent high priest caused Israel to see little lasting peace during his last years of service and thereafter for more than twenty years. Judgment because of this became inevitable, starting with the head and working its way down.

Chapter Eight
Samuel's New Era, Priestly Prophetics

s the sun sets on Eli's ministry, it is rising conspicuously on Samuel. God has Eli's protégé, Samuel, waiting in the wings to open His new era. His career is marked by two very striking states of affairs. First, there were only a few prophecies published or disseminated to the land for decades. The scripture says in 1 Samuel 3:1 that the word of the Lord was rare in those days. Second, the lamp of God's house was out. See 1 Samuel 3:3. Apparently, Eli no longer thought it important to keep it lit, so the Ark of God sat in darkness in God's tabernacle until it was captured by the Philistines. In Eli's state of mind, he would have thought, "What's the point? Why should I keep the Lord's lamp lit? Why be concerned about the Ark of the Covenant sitting in darkness?" With much of the nation serving other gods, only a few showed up to pay Yahweh homage or to worship him

anyway. Besides, the Lord had long since quit talking, and if He did, who would hear or care to listen outside of a handful of underground prophets and a few faithful saints? After all, Eli himself had no longer listened to, or for, God, so why should they? Perhaps extinguishing the lamp in God's tabernacle that priests were to keep glowing perpetually was his sons' doing. Maybe they felt it was ludicrous to waste oil keeping the light of God's habitation glowing around the clock. Whatever the case, both incidents make profoundly prophetic statements.

It appears that during Eli's waning years, the only one in the temple at Shiloh that had any interaction with the Lord was Samuel. It is evident that the Lord allowed only Eli's priestly skill and wisdom to penetrate the boy's soul over the years. In spite of all the darkness that surrounded him, Samuel did not surrender to his mentor's spiritual and moral decay. Somehow, the Lord kept Samuel shielded and pure as he grew up. Regardless of all of his flaws and failures, there appears to have been a strong bond between Eli and Samuel because when the Lord summoned the young man to His service, Samuel thought it was Eli calling at first. After a couple more times of Samuel running to him in answer to God's call, Eli's mental stupor and spiritual haze finally lifts enough to realize that his protégé was ready to be used of the Lord. When Samuel ran to him the last time, he told him how to respond to the Lord's call. Samuel obeyed and the Lord reiterated the word that he had given the first prophet that spoke to Eli in 1 Samuel 3:12. Eli accepted the reiterated word from Samuel and acknowledged that it came from the Lord, because he had heard it all before. His response was admirable, probably the last admirable thing that Eli did in his career, other than properly rear Samuel for God's use.

Example 2: King Saul's Silent Treatment

The next example of the Lord's silent treatment is Saul, Israel's first king. We talked about him earlier, but there is more to be learned from his inclusion in scripture. Saul too learned how sad it is to lose God's communion and the pain of living with His silence. Global theocracy was giving way to monarchy so that deities as sovereigns were no longer the people's choice. Working with the changing times on earth, God obviously foresaw their request and obliged them as a sign of an inevitable world transition. The time had come for Him to shift His nation from its historical and predominately divine governance to a conspicuously human one. Taking the lead in the situation to maintain His Alpha and Omega status, God permits His theocracy to defer to a human monarchy. Saul was the people's choice, more or less. They wanted a visible king and submitted their request to Samuel, their national prophet, for one.

Much to Samuel's dismay, God obliged His people and granted their request. He personally selected a king for them that would meet with their approval. The people essentially described what they wanted in a monarch, intimating how they wanted their king to look and act. He was to be just like the monarchs of other nations around them. The Lord instructed Samuel to install the king they wanted. Later Samuel finds out that Israel's first king is to be Saul, son of Kish. Before giving them the king after their own heart, God instructs Samuel to warn His people of what life would be like under a mortal king. He wants it to be a matter of record so that they would later discern His excellence from human frailty. Despite the somberness of Samuel's words, the people continued to demand a king over them, like the nations who were ruled by them. In acquiescing to their demand for a human king, the Lord chose Saul to grant their petition. He permitted, and over time tolerated, Saul's kingship to show His people that they could not judge a book by its cover. God knew the man would be a dismal failure, but they would not believe Him, even with Him telling them in advance everything their new king would do to them.

Saul just could not get the hang of being Yahweh's monarch, even though Samuel instructed him on how to rule as God's royal representative. Saul, as history shows, promptly became the people's king, yet he never could quite get hold of ruling under God. He fell into the customary way kings reigned at the time. Wholly narcissistic, Saul lived and reigned for himself and for popular approval. Both became his ruin. The people's feelings, criticisms, complaints and desires consumed him until he lost both his high standing with God spiritually and his throne to David eventually.

Saul's First Assignment and Big Mistake

The Lord tested His new king by giving him express orders regarding a critical military campaign. Saul was to conquer King

Agag and all of his land, leave nothing alive, and take nothing from the slaughter. The king, of course, modified God's commands to suit the will of the people and to accommodate his own selfishness. Saul kept some prize livestock and brought home the king alive as both a trophy and perhaps an alliance or coach. God reacted to Saul's disobedience by condemning it. In response, he blamed his failure on the people's whims to exonerate himself for disobeying His God. He claimed he altered the Lord's directives to give the people what they wanted. To obey his subjects, Saul sacrificed his standing with the Lord and in due course closed God's mouth and wisdom to him in the end. Thus began Saul's demise. God cut off communications with him, literally fired him shortly after his inauguration. However, it took the Lord twenty years to get the irresponsible king off his throne because He had first to get His successor ready to reign in his place.

From the moment the Lord severed relations and communications with Saul, he was forced to lead Israel without the Almighty's guidance. Quickly he felt God's distance from the throne and launched a futile quest to regain His favor. Along the way, he lost his mind, assassinated the Lord's priests, and committed a host of other unforgivable atrocities against His nation's God and its ministers. Eventually, Saul was compelled to confront how poorly equipped he was to do his job without the God that put him into power. It became plain to him that forfeiting the Lord's divine intervention, wisdom, or insight by putting the people over their God was a grave mistake; one from which he would never recover. The result of his bad judgment meant Saul ruled in spiritual darkness for the rest of his reign.

The day before Saul's death, he anguished over the fact that the darkness he once enjoyed to be free of God's involvement in his rule was now destroying him. Samuel, who had attempted to guide Saul in God's stead in his early years, ignored Saul until his death. It was also glaringly evident that the other prophets, aware of the Lord's issues with Saul, followed suit. They too refused to speak to Saul, even though he was their king, which is probably why they stayed underground in fear of their lives. They knew Saul was vicious and vengeful; he had killed the Lord's priests in his fury. The prophets probably concluded that it would have been foolish for them to attempt to prophesy to Saul because of his temper, and because the Lord was most likely not saying anything to them about him anyway, at least anything they wanted to prophesy to an insane king. In any case, the witches, wizards, diviners, and magicians had assumed their duties.

Frustrated, Israel's first king found he could not get any reliable spiritual guidance from anywhere in his realm. His only source of divine information was the darkness that he had worshipped for so long and pretended to banish. Saul's diminished influence with God and His agents of light reached its peak. At a critical do-or-die moment in his reign, he was forced to resort to a witch to learn how his impending military campaign would fare. Saul also wanted to know what would befall his nation and what would become of him and his rule. Pathetically, his last official act before going to the war that would end his life was to go to the witch of Endor to find out how it would all turn out. He desperately wanted to know if he would win or loose. Saul's hopelessness drove him to the other side because if Yahweh would never speak to him again, he was certain that He would not help him win a war. Yet, the Most High was all he had left to turn to in his darkest hour. To learn his fate, the king sought the darkness, and the message he received in return scared him witless.

Saul Visits a Witch for a Prophecy

The Witch of Endor, with little coaching, obliges Saul to perform a séance to bring Samuel up from the grave. It was a horrible request, but Saul was doomed and desperate. The witch, on the other hand, was motivated by different factors altogether. After all, Saul was the king and such a request could hardly be refused. Besides, the notoriety that could come from doing a special favor for the king was worth a great deal in public relations and increased business. And then there was the subtle promise of the king's endorsement of all the demonic powers and agencies in the land if he liked what she did for him. The opportunities and possibilities were just too promising to pass up. She risked her own safety since the king had come to her; she had no longer feared for her life. That was reason enough for her to believe that her service to the king would materialize special rewards for her. She was, after all, pleasing the highest power in the land.

So the witch accommodates the king and brings up Samuel, whom Saul asks her to summon from the grave. She was apparently not too well versed in Israel's historical back-story because she seemed not to recognize the name of the person that Saul wanted her to bring up from the dead. Perhaps she felt that Saul meant someone else, certainly not the great Prophet Samuel who no doubt would have been known by her in his lifetime. Another possibility is that she never truly thought that Samuel would appear. In any case, the witch worked her magic and incantations and succeeded in raising Samuel's spirit and mantle from the grave. As stunned as anyone when the old prophet Samuel appeared before them, the witch quickly recovers from her shock and retreats to allow Samuel's spirit and Saul to talk. Discreetly she withdraws until the two men complete their business, and what a tragic business it turned out to be.

Samuel started by rebuking Saul for bothering him. He expressed his annoyance at being forced to prophesy to a man from the grave that he had ignored in life. Nonetheless, Samuel was at the behest of the witch that brought him up and was forced to answer Saul's questions[66]. Samuel's prophecy, however, was not good. God's anger with Saul was never going to subside. Saul was not going to win his impending war, and within twenty-four hours, Saul and his sons were going to join Samuel in the grave. Whew! What an experience that must have been. It was so overwhelming to Saul that he passed out when the exchange was over, weakened by the entire ordeal. Clearly, the Lord used the opportunity to vent His wrath with Saul one last time and to

---

[66] Jesus had not yet closed that gate and retrieved the keys of hell, death, and the grave as it is today.

notify him that his time on Israel's throne, and earth, had come to an end, for him and his sons. Royalty would pass from the tribe of Benjamin to Judah because God never wanted any of Saul's progeny on His throne again. Lastly, his replacement David, the man after His own heart, was ready to take the reigns.

Because the Lord went silent on him, King Saul was forced to reverse himself on a very critical issue, and if that were not bad enough, his reversal caused his nation to be more vulnerable to spiritual assault than ever. Saul had banished all of the witches and wizards from the land. Heretofore, they had to ply their crafts outside the city limits. Now after all of the mayhem he had committed against the Lord, he added this one to the list as well: he overturned his own edict and visited a witch. His downward spiral just would not stop. Scripture is full of times when the Lord just could (or would) not communicate with His people. As we learned from Micah 3:6-7 earlier His doing so is tantamount to the sun going down on a messenger or minister. Considering the times, this passage suggests that the Lord closed down His entire spiritual communication network, except for the few specially selected voices that He trusted.

Chapter Nine
The Lord Turns Out the Light

What one should understand from Saul's example is that the Lord's prophets are never the only ones speaking for a deity and that is where forced divination can enter. Whenever God said that He would cease to speak to His prophets, He meant that He would not be among the divine voices broadcasting throughout His land. Prophets would continue to speak during His blackout, they just would not be His prophets, and thus their hearers would not be privy to the Almighty's mind or will on earth's matters. True information from Him would be limited to a small group of trustworthy voices. Otherwise, for all intents and purposes, the Lord would be silent to the rest of the world. In such an environment, whatever the masses heard would seem like God's words, as in the cases of Eli and Saul, but it would take the true vessels of God's voice to expose the difference.

When God Goes Silent

For the Lord to refuse to speak to His prophet, and for His people to not know when or even that He has done so, is a sign of mass judgment against a land and its people. God is somewhat doing that today. In many areas He is systematically shutting down the voices of those messengers who are speaking by the fallen spirits (angels) they have covenanted with to worship and serve in His place. This temptation is ever present with prophetic ministers. It even came as the Lord Jesus' first challenge. If you will recall, the devil came to tempt Him just before His presentation to Israel. The Messiah, however, knew His enemy, understood his motives, and defeated him with what He knew to be most effective: the Word of God. Many of today's prophetic voices and ministers in general are not as formidable in God's truth as the Messiah was, although by His Holy Spirit, we all have the opportunity to be.

When the Lord goes silent on His prophets, few of them survive the shock and pain. They know when it happens because the silence is louder than any sound they hear. In crowds, at special events, and most notably at special times where the prophet remembers enjoying unusual communion with the Lord, He is agonizingly silent. If this happens to a bona fide prophet, you will know it; you will see it in the prophet's eyes and hear its forlorn echo in the messenger's voice, if you are spiritually astute. Without words and often without admitting it, such prophets express their longing to hear the Lord's voice once more, thinking what they would not give to go back and do it all over again now that they know the sorrow of living in His silence. Gripped in the vacuum of the Lord's refusal to communicate with them, such prophets' dreams take on a dark, muted character as they inwardly realize the spiritual faculties that once served the true and living God are now being seized by another deity. The experience is much like the evil spirit that gripped Saul at will and the exact opposite of what happened to Balaam, who started out as a diviner and experienced the true ministry of the Almighty[67]. Prophets locked in the Lord's incommunicado discover their prophecies, when they can be detected, are superficial. Shallowness surrounds much of what they say. Their words make no sense and there is a tinge of anger or animosity beneath them. Prophecies from these messengers fail to connect with anything biblical or God. They are disjointed, irrelevant, and often incomprehensible or errant. Attempts to draw on the Bible only produce unrelated scripture fragments that render their prophecies unproductive and impotent. Usually their words are confusing and leave the hearer with more questions than answers; or worse, panicked. They are panicked because their predictions or insights are filled with a fleshly mysticism that strikes the new creation spirit as dangerous, even if the hearer cannot say why. Humanism, worldliness, and self-aggrandizement are the spirits behind shutout prophets' words. That is all they have left to call upon for otherworldly information.

As the total antithesis of what the Spirit of God and Christ would say or inspire, false prophecy becomes the standard communication of shutout ministers and the bane of true

---

[67] See Numbers 24.

prophecy. Prophets languishing under God's dead silence feel dead and empty inside all the time. It is why their prophetic ministrations lack the fertile enlightenment that comes from the Lord. Emptiness, a vacuous emptiness, engulfs their souls as they float through ministry trying to convince themselves that they are okay with the Lord's inaccessibility and indifference to them. They overcompensate for it by attempting to persuade others that what is lacking in their mantle's service is really not that important; it is not that deep. Those who notice and comment on it, they label as just legalistic and religious. Silenced prophets, in comparison, are free in Jesus. They are unencumbered by rules, regulations, and tradition. These messengers excessively promote liberty and grace and downplay holiness and righteousness as bondage. They mangle God's truth and claim it is subject to what they perceive as His highest law: love. Often they mean self-love and love of self, and not the Lord's love at all. To make those who follow them hardened to the Holy Spirit's conviction and partake of God's silence with them, these people overemphasize fun in Jesus and disdain sobriety. They mock and scorn seriousness in the things of God as pretentious or exaggerated spirituality. It should come as no surprise then, that they use these tactics. History shows how they replenish their followers when the true ones who discern their problems with the Lord abandon them. With their unenlightened followers gone, they cull the kingdom for deluded replacements; after all, misery does love company. Generally speaking, the out-of-the-spotlight habits of the shutout prophet fall into two extremes. Some such prophets find themselves unavoidably antagonistic with their genuine counterparts. Others enjoy sitting with them musing over their dynamics with the Lord, wistfully remembering when they were in that place with God. Either way, one thing is common to both groups: the pain of God's detachment haunts them. It never diminishes, and it will never go away until He resumes communication with them.

It is no joking matter to have the Lord go silent with any of His children, but it is a pitiful sight to witness the effects of His doing so with a prophet. There just is no sadder—sometimes madder—servant on the planet. Take care that you do not trivialize your now vibrant relations with God. If you are a prophet, make sure you build within yourself reliable boundaries and alarms to alert you to when you are crossing that dangerous line with Him. Do not let your frustration, disappointment or anger tempt you to so offend or isolate God that He ceases to reach out to you. No matter how hurtful life can be, its worst is nothing compared to being banished to the Lord's silence for the rest of your life or service with Him. It is hard to take after you have known and delighted in Him.

Chapter Ten
The 20/12 Rules

What to Do When the Silence First Happens

There may be times when you notice a lull in your communications and communion with the Lord. This happens periodically to everyone. Just because you hit a silence period with the Lord, it does not mean you and the Lord have a problem. However, you still want to address it if it goes past a certain time, like for instance a week or so. You may be too busy, too engrossed in a project, or just too embroiled in a trial to maintain your usual intensity of communion with the Lord. He understands, even if it bothers Him to be set aside by you at these times. Nonetheless, His reactions in these instances are not cases of judgment unless they drag on for months or years. God may simply be giving you the space you need to clear your world from the unexpected, temporary, or overwhelming things that hit us all on occasion. You should not, however, permit them to turn into more than that—temporary overwhelming circumstances. The typical prophet though, is attuned to these times and will usually not allow them to drag on because he or she simply cannot tolerate any extended silence from the Lord.

If you notice that the Lord persists in His silent treatment, check yourself, check your doctrine, check your routine, check your prophecies and explore their sources. Also, review your previous behavior and conduct with Him. Here are some good places to begin to explore the problem before you conclude that it is judgment or that the Lord is just being irrational, vindictive, or difficult. Below are twenty questions to ask yourself to help you chip away at God's wall of silence.

20 Questions

Breaking Through the Lord's Wall of Silence

1. Was there a time when God called you to fellowship and you purposely delayed or dismissed the call, again and again and again? How often had that been happening before the silence began?

2. Did the Lord give you an assignment that you neglected to do or failed to carry out the way He told you? Have you been dodging Him to avoid His correction in that or any other matter?

3. Do you have new relationships in your life that are eating away at your devotional time or enticing you to forego your customary intimacy or fellowship with the Lord? Remember, He is a jealous God.

4. Are you nursing hurts or pains, embittered about a trial or disappointment, or frustrated about what you feel is an outstanding promise or unanswered prayer request you feel the Lord ignored?

5. Do you refuse to be delivered by the Holy Spirit of resentment because you feel justified in your attitude? Are you maybe inwardly blaming Him for the situation?

6. Do you harbor negative emotions about God and your service that have begun to seethe and cause you to diminish your previously positive view of His goodness, righteousness or holiness? Do you voice these emotions to others, or worse yet, your family and friends?

7. Have you fallen into disrespecting the Lord due to commonizing what He says when He speaks? Do you have people in your life who are inspiring this attitude in you? Are you in relationship with people who dislike your God or scorn your relationship with Him?

8. Have you grown casual about the Lord's overtures, or begun to be ashamed of the nature of your relationship with Him especially in public among popular or prestigious friends or acquaintances?

9. How about your study times? Have you cut back on the time you used to spend studying or replaced it with something else that competes with (or unsettles) God's influence in your life?

10. Do you have an outstanding obedience that you are going to get around to fulfilling when things get right? For example, like helping someone He wants to touch through you, or forgiving someone some hurt, or

maybe getting behind someone who is not your first choice for support or aid?

11. Are you under the right leadership? Are you under a leader or in a church where the Lord is free to speak and to act? Is His word respected or suppressed where you worship? Are His prophets silenced or banished? Some churches do not have an open heaven over them that allows the Lord to speak regardless of how large or influential they may be. Often if there is no open heaven in your place of worship, it will carry over into your prayer and devotional experiences elsewhere and you will find that the Lord will not say much or anything until you get to where His voice is welcome.

12. How about your ministry's doctrines? Do they uphold or ridicule the voice of God, His will and involvement in people's lives? Are you being nurtured by ministers who do the same thing? Are you too independent of God in your thoughts, decisions, or wisdom to appreciate His word in your life?

13. Are you studying under or being mentored by people that do not respect the word or voice of the Lord? Do they ridicule intimacy with Him? Are you mocked or scorned for valuing God's input in your life and chided as being am overly religious or immature Christian because of it? If so, such attitudes are slowly likely to silence His voice to you as well.

14. How about prophecy? Do you find that you pick and choose the prophecies you want to regard based on how you feel at the time or what you want to hear from the Lord?

15. How about your prayer life in general? Is it stagnant? Do you wait too late to begin prayer and then are too

sleepy to finish? Are you closed to expanding or varying your routine prayer habits and keep the exact words and petitions of your devotions mechanical? Are you in the rut of repeating the same prayers the same way day after day? Have you done so for years with no variation?

16. Are you called to ministry and refuse to go because of work, family, history, or just plain fear? Have you tried to appease God with charitable deeds to trade off what He really wants of you?

17. How about your spiritual and moral conduct? Are you in ungodly relationships, moral uncleanness or sexual impurity?

18. What about your spiritual purity? Are you dabbling in occult activities or seeking to blend Jesus Christ with the gods and religions of this world? Sometimes an obsession with a particular genre of movie, entertainment, or habit can so turn God off that He withdraws until you are ready to let it go.

19. Do you have outstanding vows to the Lord that you began to honor and then dropped for various reasons? Do you owe Him unpaid or unfulfilled pledges, offerings, or promised sacrifices or duties?

20. Is there unforgiveness in your heart, broken promises to others, or someone you hurt and that you refuse to apologize to and repent? Are you angry with God punishing Him for something He did not do for you that you wanted?

As you can see, before things get dire, there is much you can do to take care of your relationship with the Lord. You do not have to sit by idly hoping for the best. You can take the first step, and the second and the third until God finally responds. Always reach out to God yourself. If it takes days, months or years, believe me, He is worth it. Be determined, tenacious, and relentless with God. He desires for you to pursue Him and when you catch Him, to cling to Him. Do all it takes to convince the Lord that you are serious about your relationship with Him, and show Him how determined you are by not giving up until He resumes your normal communion. Only do not play games with God; He truly detests folly and will not be conned no matter how much you have convinced yourself that you are sincere, when in reality you are not. If you are not ready to give it all you have to give, then do not initiate a level of interaction with Him that you are unprepared to maintain. Wait until you are, and in the meantime be reverent and respectful. Show your commitment to His will and good pleasure by fulfilling your duties to the Lord. Avoid demanding Him or pushing Him to do what you want, regardless of His will or wisdom on the matter. Allow your union with the Lord to progress at His pace. He knows how much you can bear and that includes the weight of His glory. Do not make rash vows or pretentious public declarations about how you will die for the Lord, when you are not yet ready to live for Him as He desires. Treat Him as He is, the Almighty. God is all seeing, all knowing, and everywhere present at once, so act like it. Do not hide from Him or behave as if He needs your confession to know what you are into or what is going on with you. Be open and frank with God, as the God of truth He dislikes lies of any kind no matter what form or color they take. Above all believe that the Lord is all the God that He says He is.

After all of this information, would it not also be good to know how to talk with God and the most effective ways to commune with Him? Here are some tips that might guide your future communications with your heavenly Father and your Lord and Savior Jesus Christ.

Recently, in one of my mid-week services, I asked the church what they thought would cause the Lord to go silent on them. The best answer came from one of my young ones. The youngster was eleven and he said that "if you discourage the Lord He may not want to talk to you anymore." They had been learning about prophets and prophecy, believe it or not from my book, *The Prophet's Dictionary*. Truly, a little child shall lead you. We as adults are so familiar with the Lord and presumptuous in our treatment of Him that we cannot fathom that the Lord can become discouraged with us. Yet He said that we could weary Him with our behaviors and grieve His Holy Spirit. In particular, we can weary Him with our misconduct, indifference, and impudence. These are just as discouraging to Him as they would be to us, since we are indeed made in His image and likeness. Below are twelve ideas on how not to so discourage the Lord that He refuses to respond to you any longer. Below are some other tips on building and maintaining a powerful relationship with the Almighty.

12 Tips to Get & Keep the Lord Talking

1. Start with a desire to listen. This sounds easier than it is because cultivating an ear to hear God takes work, consistency and patience. Be courteous to the Lord, and attentive when He speaks. This takes practice, as we naturally want to cut Him off when He begins to speak to take over the conversation. It is common for us as humans to interrupt God when He starts to speak because our own spirits and souls get so excited that they jump in before He gets more than a few words out. Restrain this impulse and correct it when it happens.

2. Know the Lord your God. This requires knowing His Word, the entire scripture. Often people want to hear from God in contemporary form and forget that many voices have gone out into the world that pretend to be His. You must develop sifters and filters that screen out what is God from the myriad of other voices competing for your spiritual ear, attention and worship.

3. Take some classes on the Holy Spirit, spiritual gifts, and basic prophetics to learn the patterns and methods of divine communication. The good classes will include some study of dreams and visions, symbolism, and God's parabolic communications. In particular, study prophecy and not just the modern kind, but also the prophecies of scripture to learn how God thinks, acts, and communicates. This will help you discern Him from other

spiritual voices. All classes should be based on His word and not just traditional or contemporary church theology, or popular books on the subject. You want to be sure to have a good Bible foundation before enrolling in these classes because once you enter that realm, all kinds of supernatural forces will attempt to woo you to seize your spiritual communications channel. Be thoughtful and take your time to learn the voice of your God; it really is quite distinct when you pay attention.

4. Be quick to hear and obey. It is commendable that people want to talk with the Lord, but God is still who He is. He expects to be obeyed and not trifled with or faked. If you are not prepared to go the distance with Him, then put off your press into the spirit until you are better equipped for it.

5. Reverence the Lord; hallow your God and your Redeemer in your heart. Approach the Lord as the Almighty Creator of heaven and earth, not just your casual buddy or pal. Despite the fact that He made you His child, irreverence and casualness are still deep affronts to His Person. Peter tells us in 1 Peter 3:15 to sanctify the Lord in our hearts. That means treating Him differently and better than you treat or think of everyone else. Remember that God is the Maker of all other gods. So do not treat Him as you would one of His angels or fallen spirits or even your most beloved person on earth.

6. Believe that He is. Hebrews 11:6 says, *"But without faith it is impossible to please him: for he that cometh to God must believe that He is, and that He is a rewarder of them that diligently seek Him."* Two things are noteworthy in this passage. One is the word "diligent". It is not as passive as the modern church presents it. The diligence the Lord is talking about here involves searching out everything that you can get your hands on about the Lord, His Son our Redeemer, and their lifestyle. Diligent search requires investigating and proving all that you uncover about them is truth, and not just information or knowledge. The Lord wants you to crave Him, so be conscientious about the time you schedule for Him. The very nature of your fellowship and communion with the Lord rests on His not being postponed for anything if you can help it. Our God responds when you do all you can to seek Him carefully, consistently and worshipfully. And then there is the word "rewarder". Here the sentiment is that God will back you, deliver you, perform His good word to you, recompense and restore you. Once He is content with you, He will sway His seen and unseen powers for you. When you diligently seek and continually hallow Him as your first priority and not last resort, God has no problem releasing all of His covenant blessings on your life without your begging, pleading and fasting to persuade Him.

7. Answer the Lord. Be there for Him if you want Him to be there for you, and be prompt about it.

8. Give God's issues, concerns, and interests first place in your life. Do not fall into the trap of giving Him excuses when He calls on you to do something for Him, or begging off when He reaches out to you.

9. Be scrupulous about Matthew 6:33. Do not just seek the Lord, pray for a prophecy or a word, or appeal to Him just to get your needs met. Avoid settling into empty devotional communions with the Lord. Seek first His entire kingdom and its righteousness. Know what righteousness is and means to the Lord and do not assume that just because He saved you that there is no longer anything unrighteous about you. Know God's world; be interested in His issues, and sensitive to His duties and responsibilities to the whole planet and not just your piece of it.

10. Be circumspect in all your conduct. Many times the Lord will refuse to respond to our overtures because there are things we do that discredit Him. Sometimes sin is not just what you do that is immoral or unethical; these are not the only issues God has with humanity on earth. There are things that you can do that the world approves that discredit the Lord and His righteousness, violate His law of truth, or simply dismiss Jesus Christ. It is pretty difficult to appeal to someone for help that you have publicly ridiculed, profaned or disowned. Live in public as if God is in the flesh with you. There are many things that you restrain yourself from doing to your carnal friends, family

or acquaintances purely on the basis of your relationship with them, and because they are present in the flesh. Your love, admiration or plain old need for them keeps you from misrepresenting them to your world. The Lord expects that same kind of regard and emotional restraint.

11. Be a child of faith and childlike in your faith. Approach God on the terms that He appointed for all creation, which is faith. Believe in Him, but also believe in what He believes in and stands for as well. The Lord has lived a long time, outlasting all of His opposers and adversaries. As Creator He owns and rules everything in His worlds. He managed to build and sustain a kingdom that is unrivaled and unparalleled by anything His creaturehood can attempt in all His worlds. He has economized planets, sustained nations, and continues to populate His created and uncreated worlds. If for no other reason than these achievements, He is worthy of honor and respect. Accepting these realities at face value is the ultimate test and act of your faith. Setting out to search His word and compare it with these realities is the greatest sign of allegiance to Him. If God is worthy of your attention, then He is doubly worthy of your convictions. Be persuade in your own heart of who and what He is. Truly, the phrase, "worship the Lord for all that He has done" is essential to gaining God's ear. The word "done" there would be stated in our times this way: "Worship the Lord for all of His achievements and accomplishments."

12. Do not just pencil God into your busy life. Have a set time where He can count on your being there when He comes to you. Prayer on the run may be unavoidable at times, but communion should be planned and observed according to a regular schedule. Also, commune with God alone and not with friends. Public worship is normal but communion deserves private devotions. Avoid needing a companion to help you seek and reach God. In addition, do not permit others to tell you how it must be with God. After you have learned Him, He will tell you Himself what He likes and dislikes during His times with you and how He desires you to approach and fellowship with Him as His child.

The most important tip of all is this one: Do not confuse or blend the Lord with other gods. Without question, resume for resume, accomplishment for accomplishment, He outstrips them all hands down. The next time you want to compare the gods of this world with your God, the Most High, just look at their records. You can learn a great deal about deities by simply examining their records as seen in their histories and the lifestyles of their people. Many of the gods competing with the Lord Jesus Christ today have a proven track record of failure. Look at their nations, the poverty of their people, the inequities and instabilities of their governments. Think about this, would you really hire a person to rule another country that could not even bring his or her own people out of darkness, poverty, despair, and primitivity? Gods should, and in many ways do, apply for their posts. They subtly present their accomplishments and abilities just like humans. Since their world systems predate ours it is wise to look at what they have done with what they had in the way of human and natural resources.

I regularly look at the record of the deities rivaling Jesus Christ and think to myself, "These beings have not helped or lifted up their own nations, and now they want to takeover mine." For all that may be wrong with the lands the Most High founded and rules, their prosperity, innovation and ingenuity, and overall climate still remains the envy of the others.

Below is a recollection of how I have successfully kept the Lord walking and talking with me for nearly 30 years. There is not a single day that goes by that I do not hear the Lord and richly enjoy His companionship in my life. My secrets for how to do so come after years of knowing and passionately loving Him. For me it all started in my early years with the Lord. Upon my salvation and the baptism of the Holy Spirit, I immediately enjoyed great communion with Him. God spoke to me incessantly, as He still does, about everything. Not a day went by nor did an evening close without Him sharing His thoughts with me on different things. After awhile it became a habit and I grew accustomed to it. I relished it and depended on it. Suddenly one day I heard nothing. He did not talk, think, or express any feeling at all. It was as if a wall of silence came down between us and I was disturbed. Being new to it all I felt that perhaps God just needed time because I did not know what to make of His abrupt silence.

The first day went by and I did not do anything. I just waited for the next day, assuming He would resume our lifestyle then. He did not. I waited all day long and nothing happened. The third day came and the silence got deafening. I felt His distance between us thickening, so I broke it myself because I was frustrated. Something inside me told me that He was testing me – I cannot tell you what that was; it just became clear. After I got hold of that idea, I simply said to the Lord out loud, "I know You are testing me to see if I would miss You if You did not speak to me one day. I want You to know now that You can end Your test. I will miss You and would if we did not speak for a whole day or for a long while in a day. I want You to talk to me all day everyday whenever You have something to say, and I want that to be our covenant." I heard nothing in return, but the next morning things were back to normal and it has been that way ever since. The remedy to your situation, if there is a divine wall of silence in your life, may be just that simple.

I am aware that many people do not want such intimate involvement with the Lord. They would prefer to have to deal with Him that way after they leave this world. He understands and accepts it. Such preferences do not diminish His love for them, or cause Him to care for or tend to people like that any less. On the other hand, there are those who crave such closeness with the Lord because He created us for it. God is very relational. He is family oriented and wants His children to visit and commune with Him often as any parent does. That is why when He has to silence Himself with any one of them, it saddens Him. If you will remember, Jesus was very sociable on earth. He loved to fellowship, to visit people, and to dine with them. He was so sociable that His adversaries took issue with it. They could not understand how He could be as powerful, holy, and intelligent as He was and do all that He did and still want to spend time with the common people they despised. Their distaste did not bother our Lord. He just kept being Himself and loving His people. That is why He and His Father created them in the first place. Jesus loved to feast and fellowship with people and delighted in entertaining the souls He made for He and His Father's enjoyment. It was something that He longed for way before He became flesh. For His brief time on earth, He was able to do so as one of them, so to speak, and He rejoiced in it.

None of that has changed for the Lord; He still enjoys the company of His family. He takes pleasure in our worship, is pleased when we invite Him to our celebrations, weddings, and family events. The Lord gets pleasure from our gifts and loves to hear our hearts, our hopes, and our dreams. Spending time with us is what God looks forward to, and we are never boring to Him. He does not dread our coming, nor is He irked by the sound of our voices. He loves being a Dad and helping us work out our lives. When and if the Lord clearly demonstrates that He does not wish to deal with you, you may have to dig deeper and work harder at regaining your special place with Him. In the meantime, and in the process, do not allow theology, tradition, or other people's inability to reciprocate to Him hinder you from partaking of the best thing God has to offer: *Himself.*

About the Author

Paula A. Price is a strong and widely acknowledged international voice on the subject of apostolic and prophetic ministry. She is recognized as a modern-day apostle with a potent prophetic anointing. Active in full-time ministry since 1985, she has founded and established three churches, an apostolic and prophetic Bible institute, a publication company, consulting firm, and global collaborative network linking apostles and prophets together for the purpose of kingdom vision and ventures. Through this international ministry, she has transformed the lives of many through her wisdom and revelation of God's kingdom.

As a former sales and marketing executive, Dr. Price effectively blends ministerial and entrepreneurial applications in her ministry to enrich and empower a diverse audience with the skills and abilities to take kingdoms for the Lord Jesus Christ. A lecturer, teacher, curriculum developer and business trainer, Dr. Price globally consults Christian businesses, churches, schools and assemblies. Over a 20-year period, Dr. Price has developed a superior curriculum to train Christian ministers and professionals, particularly the apostle and the prophet. Her programs often are used in both secular and non-secular environments worldwide. Although she has written over 25 books, manuals, and other course material on the apostolic and prophetic, she is most recognized for her unique 1,600-term *Prophet's Dictionary*, and her concise prophetic training manual entitled *The Prophet's Handbook*. Other releases include *Divine Order for Spiritual Dominance*, a five-fold ministry tool, and *Eternity's Generals*, an explanation of today's apostle.

Beyond the pulpit, Dr. Price is the provocative talk show host of her own program, *Let's Just Talk: Where God Makes Sense.* She brings the pulpit to the pew, weekly applying God's wisdom and divine pragmatism to today's world solutions. Her ministry goal is to make Christ's teachings and churches relevant for today. "Eternity in the Now" is the credo through which she accomplishes it.

In addition to her vast experience, Dr. Price has a D.Min. and a PhD in Religious Education from Word of Truth Seminary in Alabama. She is also a wife, mother of three daughters, and the grandmother of two. She presently pastors New Creation Worship Assembly in Broken Arrow, OK.

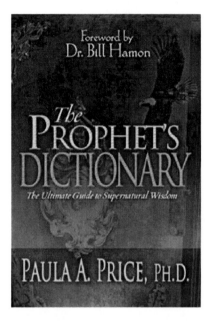

THE PROPHET'S DICTIONARY

The Ultimate Guide to Supernatural Wisdom

The Prophet's Dictionary by Paula Price is an essential tool for laymen, prophets, prophesiers, pastors, intercessors, and dreamers of dreams. As an all-in-one dictionary and reference book containing over 1,600 relevant definitions of terms and phrases for the prophetic realm of Christian ministry, it exposes ancient religious seductions and how they have infiltrated movies, television, and books. Prophetic visions and clues to interpreting their symbolism, imagery, and signs are also included.

$25.95

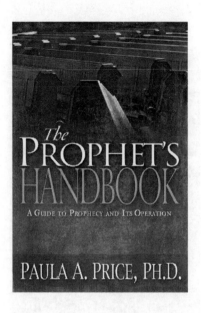

THE PROPHET'S HANDBOOK

A Guide to Prophecy and Its Operation

The Prophet's Handbook: A Guide to Prophecy and Its Operation by Dr. Paula A. Price is a companion text to the acclaimed, *The Prophet's Dictionary: The Ultimate Guide to Supernatural Wisdom*. *The Prophet's Handbook* details the roles and duties of the prophetic in the church and clearly explains its necessity. As an indispensable reference, this comprehensive text is something no church leader should be without. Dr. Paula Price intelligently and skillfully explains the function and responsibilities of local church prophets and those who prophesy. Her years of research and ministry have led to the ultimate guide to prophecy in the local church.

$16.99

troducing the Standardized Ministry Assessment Series
ɔw do I test my Spiritual IQ?

ɘ our standardized ministry assessments to help determine where you fit—whether ninistry or business; find out how equipped you are for your calling, and evaluate ɪr readiness. Our assessments are essential tools for Christian ministry that aid in ɪessing the potential and proficiency of those claiming or exhibiting ministerial ɪtude or giftings in action.

rpose for Destiny (PFD)

ɪe you ever asked yourself, *"What was God thinking when He made me?"* Are you a leader ɪ members who seem like square pegs in round holes? If so, the **Purpose for Destiny ɘstionnaire** is ideal for you or your team.

ɪistry Assessment Questionnaire (MAQ)

ɪ MAQ is for any minister, leader, or gifted individual called to serve. It is an ɘssment created to identify the various features of five-fold ministry at work in an vidual, as exhibited and/or practiced by the ministries featured in Ephesians 4:11 and I ɪinthians 12:28-29.

ɪphetic Aptitude Questionnaire (PAQ)

ɪ prophets, intercessors, psalmists, seers, prayer warriors, and the like, the PAQ is an ɪuative assessment tool to help Christian leaders evaluate those entrusted to their ɪphetic oversight or tutelage and to determine where their prophetic ministers may best ve. The PAQ is ideal for individuals interested in understanding their prophetic identity.

ostolic Diagnostic Questionnaire (ADQ)

ɘ ADQ is for apostles—seasoned and new; prophets—new and veteran; and pastors and ɪrch leaders inclined to apostolic ministry. It pinpoints whether you are called to serve ɪcially in apostolic ministry or operate in the gifting. The AAQ reveals your strengths, ɪknesses, and areas that need training and development.

hat is the value of these assessments?

- Connect ministers with identity and calling
- Join leaders with a profitable tool for ministry selection
- Unite students with guidance and direction
- Link readiness programs with accurate evaluation of their trainees

For more information, visit www.drpaulaprice.com or call (877) 649-7764
to speak with an assessment representative.

More Books by Dr. Paula Price

The Prophet's Handbook

The Prophet's Handbook answers all the questions about prophecy and the prophetic that have gone unanswered for years. Find out what makes a prophet; how a prophet differs from a psychic; how God calls, awakens, and grooms excellent prophets; and how to recognize and work with prophets in the local church. $16.99

Prophecy: God's Divine Communications Media

Divine Communications helps you understand how prophecy works and why it is needed in our time. Find out why God's method of communication is superior. $14.99

Eternity's Generals: The Wisdom of Apostleship

Eternity's Generals standardizes all the Lord intends about the apostle by explaining why apostles are born and not made, and how they may be recognized by more than personal achievements. $29.95

Divine Order for Spiritual Dominance

A challenging, fresh look at the five-fold offices, *Divine Order* uses a clever combination of both teaching and study to "settle" this classic Ephesians 4:11 argument: What is God's intended order? $22.50

Money is a Spirit: The Economy Within

Money is a Spirit is the how-to, must-read of the finance world. Learn why wealth doesn't start with the dollar, it starts with the idea. $14.99

The Five-Fold Ministry Offices

The Five-Fold Ministry Offices outlines, in workbook style, the functions, traits, and attributes of each five-fold officer represented in Ephesians 4:11. $14.99

For more information, call **877-649-7764**
Or visit us online at www.drpaulaprice.com

CPSIA information can be obtained at www.ICGtesting.com
Printed in the USA
241683LV00005B/33/P